"Then **Ara** Said to **Joe**..."

The Best Notre Dame Football Stories Ever Told

John Heisler

TRIUMPH
B O O K S

Library of Congress Cataloging-in-Publication Data

Heisler, John
  Then Ara said to Joe: the best Notre Dame football stories ever told / John Heisler.
      p. cm.
  Includes bibliographical references.
  ISBN-13: 978-1-60078-002-8
  ISBN-10: 1-60078-002-4
1. Notre Dame Fighting Irish (Football team)—History. 2. University of Notre Dame—Football—History. I. Title.
  GV958.N6H44 2007
  796.332'630977289—dc22

                              2007014967

This book is available in quantity at special discounts for your group or organization. For further information, contact:

Triumph Books
542 South Dearborn Street
Suite 750
Chicago, Illinois 60605
(312) 939-3330
Fax (312) 663-3557

Printed in U.S.A.
ISBN: 978-1-60078-002-8
Design by Patricia Frey
All photos courtesy of the University of Notre Dame Sports Information Department unless indicated otherwise

To Ara Parseghian and Joe Theismann, whose names help comprise the title of this book. They distinguished themselves as coach and player, respectively, with the Irish—Parseghian as head coach from 1964 to 1974 and Theismann as an All-American quarterback from 1968 to 1970. Both are now College Football Hall of Fame inductees. More importantly, both have been exemplary representatives of Notre Dame since they left campus. And, just as importantly, their exploits with the Irish left behind the sorts of stories Notre Dame fans love to tell.

table of
contents

preface

Because only one of the two great Irish quarterbacks named Joe had the opportunity to play for Ara, Joe Theismann and Joe Montana never had the opportunity to hang out together on the University of Notre Dame campus.

Theismann graduated in 1971, and Montana showed up three falls later in 1974 as a freshman. The two came to know each other after both gained identities as standout Irish signal-callers—and stars at the professional level, as well.

And both Theismann and Montana ended up part of the lore of Notre Dame football—Theismann thanks in part to his on-field play, along with the decision to change the pronunciation of his last name from THEES-man to rhyme with Heisman; and Montana thanks to a national championship in '77, plus a series of eye-popping comebacks, including the famed chicken-soup escapade in the Cotton Bowl win over Houston that closed out his college career.

If you follow Notre Dame football, you probably know about Knute Rockne's "Win One for the Gipper" speech. You've relived the 1977 green-jersey game against USC. Then there's the Saturday afternoon in Notre Dame Stadium in 1980 when the wind apparently stopped just long enough for Harry Oliver to kick a 51-yard field goal to beat Michigan.

Thanks to the long-term success and visibility of Notre Dame football, Irish fans have never lacked for tales to relate. The coaching acumen and marketing wizardry of Knute Rockne. The Four Horsemen. The perfection of Frank Leahy and the long list of All-Americans and Heisman Trophy winners who played for him. The eras of national title architects Ara Parseghian, Dan Devine, and Lou Holtz. And the championship teams and all-star players that have been part of just about every decade in the Irish history book.

In *"Then Ara Said to Joe..."* we bring you a selection of those tales from the gridiron high points at Notre Dame. Many of them come from the pages of the Notre Dame official football game day programs, ably edited in recent years by Notre Dame sports information staffers Bernie Cafarelli (a 1983 Notre Dame graduate) and Tim Connor. Former sports information student assistants Craig Chval (a 1981 Notre Dame grad now living in Columbia, Missouri) and Ken Kleppel (a former baseball manager and 2001 Notre Dame grad) did many of the interviews and caught up with lots of the former Irish players. Both Chval and Kleppel went on to legal careers, Kleppel after graduating from Notre Dame's law school in 2004.

Lou Somogyi, longtime *Blue & Gold Illustrated* writer and editor (and a 1984 Notre Dame grad), put together the profiles of Notre Dame's Heisman Trophy winners—helped by gridiron historian and former San Diego sportswriter Bud Maloney. In between, there are lots of other nuggets, thanks to contributions from sports information staffers Connor and Chris Masters, former College Football Hall of Fame executive director Bernie Kish, former sports information intern Cory Walton, sports information student assistant Greg Touney (a 2007 Notre Dame graduate), and Kristy Katzmann (a 2000 Notre Dame grad who originally profiled Tim McCarthy for *Notre Dame Magazine*).

Check out these tales from the front lines of Notre Dame football through the years. They're likely to bring back memories of your own tales from Irish gridiron seasons of yesteryear.

chapter 1
The Knute Rockne Years

Blending candid coaching tips with acerbic wit, Knute Rockne was just as effective at using the stick as he was the carrot when motivating his players and teams.

Knute Rockne knew how to push the right buttons of his players at exactly the right time—how to motivate them, relax them, and make them more confident.

Rockne: A Line for Every Occasion

Knute Rockne, who coached the Irish from 1918 until his death following the 1930 season, was never shy about using a little sarcasm with his players to motivate them:

- To one of his better players who was struggling on the field one Saturday—"You forgot to show him your newspaper clippings. He doesn't know how good you are."
- To one of his teams that trailed at halftime of a game—"You're supposed to be the Fighting Irish? You look to me like a lot of peaceful sissies."
- On communicating with his players—"I can tell you one thing 12 times. After that, you're on your own. There are some dumb people, then some dumber ones, then you come next."
- Entering the locker room with his team behind—"Pardon me, girls, I thought this was the Notre Dame team."
- On the human nature of his players—"Sometimes they look like a million dollars, sometimes they look like a Mickey Mouse animated cartoon."
- On an afternoon when his team was struggling at home—"We're likely to lose the first game that's been lost on our home grounds in 25 years. That's a fine story you'll be able to tell your grandchildren. You once had the honor of disgracing Notre Dame."
- When a midweek scrimmage was not going as he had hoped—"Go on to the showers, boys, before Jack Cannon ruins any more plays."
- Coining a description of his 1928 team—"I call them the 'Minute Men' because they're in the game about a minute before the other team scores."
- One of his coaching philosophies—"One loss is good for the soul. Too many losses are not good for the coach."
- On one occasion on the road when his team was refused admittance at the stadium gate—"This is going to be easier than we thought, boys. They aren't expecting us."

- On what it takes to be successful—"The qualifications for a lineman are to be big and dumb. The qualifications to play in the backfield are just to be dumb."
- His appeal to help a lost soul—"Someone explain to Wilbur what this is all about. He's new—he's only been on the squad three years."
- To a particular player who missed his block twice in a row—"I'm taking you out and saving you for the junior prom."
- On the ever-present second-guessing of his decisions—"I sometimes wonder why a college hires a coach when there are so many experts in town. If I would walk into the barbershop or into a club, I would say, 'And how are all the coaches today?'"
- On particularly physical opposing players—"If your adversary persists in the delusion that he is Jack Dempsey, disillusion him."
- On priorities—"I have only one favor to ask. When crossing the goal line, please remember to take the ball with you."
- On losing a player due to academics—"Our team traveled 25,000 miles, then he fails geography."
- To a player who wasn't exerting himself enough—"Throw away your knitting needles and get in the game."
- To a player who was telegraphing plays—"It'd be better to send your opponent a postcard."
- To a player who suggested he was going to turn in his uniform—"I was about to ask for it, anyway."
- To George Gipp, who appeared Wednesday after missing Monday and Tuesday practices—"George, George, where have you been? Now get over here with the sixth team."
- When a practice was not going well—"What's wrong with you Irish? Do you work nights? You sleep out there all afternoon."
- His version of school spirit—"To hell with the guy who'll die for Notre Dame. I want men who will fight to keep it alive."

- On why being ticket manager is a thankless job—
  "Someone has to sit around the goal line or even behind
  the goal posts and what they have to say about the
  blankety-blank hound who sold them their tickets
  fortunately has never been printed."
- On springtime priorities—"I don't know whether we
  ought to have spring practice this year. It might take too
  much time from your drinking and necking."

Rockne didn't mind fabricating a story once in a while if he
thought it might help win a game. Once, prior to a game at
Georgia Tech in Atlanta, he read a telegram from his wife,
Bonnie, that referenced his son Billy. The telegram suggested
that Billy had suddenly been taken seriously ill and that the one
thing that seemed to be worrying him the most was whether or
not Daddy's team would win. Bonnie added that if the team
could manage to win the game, it might be the best thing for
poor little Billy. That's all Rockne's team needed to hear. The
Irish proceeded to crush Georgia Tech, forcing one of its backs,
Red Barron, to fumble seven different times from the force of the
Notre Dame defense.

When the Notre Dame traveling party rolled into the train
station in South Bend, there was little Billy, jumping up and down
and looking healthy as a horse. Years later, when Rockne would
run into members of that team, a common opening line would be,
"And how is your boy Bill?"

Rockne had his own way of keeping his players from becoming overconfident, despite what others might be saying about
them. On one occasion, he passed out newspapers to his team
before the game, saying, "Read these. These clippings say you're
all All-America. But you couldn't beat a team last week that had no
All-Americas. I want you to read these clippings before every play.
Either you just aren't that good, or you're yellow."

He once decided to let the team determine by vote which part
of the team was more important, the line or the backfield. The line
won, seven votes to four. "And don't you backs ever forget it," he
added.

Just in case there was a question, Rockne made certain all involved knew who was in charge. "I am running this team. Nobody else has anything to say about its makeup or play. If it's a flop, pan me. If it's a success—well, let them say what they choose. I have worked around here as an assistant for four years and seldom seen my name in print."

Rockne also understood exactly how coaches would be judged: "Someday there will be an exhibit in some American museum. It will be the forlorn figure of a coach who pleased nobody. And next to it will be another—and more forlorn exhibit—the preserved remains of the coach who tried to please everybody."

Nicknames Unlimited: The Four Horsemen

Nicknames in college football, much less in sports in general, are a dime a dozen. But maybe no nickname in all of collegiate football history has had more staying power and remains as recognizable as the Four Horsemen of Notre Dame.

The Four Horsemen were the backfield of the 1924 Notre Dame football squad—quarterback Harry Stuhldreher and backs Jim Crowley, Don Miller, and Elmer Layden. Together, they helped the Irish go unbeaten, knock off Stanford in the Rose Bowl, and claim a consensus national championship. But it was early in the '24 season, in conjunction with a 13–7 win over Army at the Polo Grounds in New York, that they earned the name that would be their claim to fame for years to come.

Covering the game in the press box for one of the New York newspapers was a sportswriter named Grantland Rice. While the game was being played, he had a conversation with a Notre Dame student publicity aide named George Strickler, who mentioned to Rice a connection to the Four Horsemen of the Apocalypse.

That day in the press box, Rice typed out what came to be the most familiar newspaper passage in football history:

"Outlined against a blue-gray October sky the Four Horsemen rode again. In dramatic lore they are known as famine, pestilence,

Long before Prime Time and other players with famous nicknames came along, the Four Horsemen of Notre Dame had already laid claim to the greatest nickname in the history of football.

destruction, and death. These are only aliases. Their real names are Stuhldreher, Miller, Crowley, and Layden."

What cemented the legacy of those four players were those words combined with what Strickler did back in South Bend once the team returned to campus. Taken by Rice's story, Strickler contacted a South Bend livery stable and borrowed four horses on which he posed the four Notre Dame players on Monday. The famed copyrighted photograph that resulted remains as identifiable as any image in sports.

Mention the Four Horsemen and sports fans young and old immediately connect the phrase with college football and Notre Dame. They may not recognize Miller or Layden, Stuhldreher or Crowley, all of them now deceased, but there's a cache to the name that has enabled them to remain legends in the college football world eight decades after they played.

Coach Knute Rockne had his own thoughts on the Fab Four:

- When the Four Horsemen got a little full of themselves in 1924—"I'm starting the first-team backfield with the second-team line. It might teach those fellows they can't do it alone."
- When it was suggested the Four Horsemen actually pose on horses—"Okay, you can put the boys aboard. But God help you if they fall off and get hurt."
- On how he may have initially misjudged the Four Horsemen—"I thought they could be whipped into a combination of average players. Not much more than that at the time. That's all the dream I had of them then."

Rockne: The Coach and the Car

In May of 1928 Knute Rockne, head football coach of the University of Notre Dame, became an employee of South Bend's famed Studebaker Corporation. This is the story of a giant of a man and his relationship with a legendary American corporation.

In early '28 South Bend was viewed as one of the most remarkable success stories in America. With a population of 126,000 people, South Bend was in many ways a miniature version of the nation's larger melting pots, including Pittsburgh, Detroit, and Cleveland.

The city by the bend of the St. Joseph River was home to more than 450 industrial establishments manufacturing more than 600 kinds of products. Companies like Oliver Chilled Plow Works, Bendix Brake, Singer Sewing Machine, Dodge Manufacturing, and South Bend Tool and Dye called South Bend home. However, the crown jewel of the bustling, diverse, and dynamic industrial community was clearly the Studebaker Corporation.

Studebaker's roots in South Bend went all the way back to 1852 when Henry and Clem Studebaker opened a small black-smith shop on Washington Street. Before long, the Studebakers were manufacturing more carriages and wagons than anyone in

America. In 1904 the company began producing automobiles. When Rockne joined the Studebaker team, the company was the 10th largest manufacturer of automobiles in the world with 30 branches, 4,000 service stations, and more than 5,000 dealers, not only in the United States but also around the world.

And who was this man Rockne, who was now, in 1928, a Studebaker man? Born in Voss, Norway, in 1888, he arrived at Notre Dame in 1910 as a 22-year-old freshman from Chicago's Scandinavian North Side. At Notre Dame, he excelled in sports as a middle distance runner and pole vaulter on the track team and captained the football team his senior year, helping lead the Irish to a 35–13 victory over Army at West Point and putting the small Catholic school on the college gridiron map. Rock, as his friends called him, also earned pin money as an amateur boxer in South Bend.

The story of Rockne and Studebaker has at its roots Rockne's relationship with Albert Erskine, president of the Studebaker Corporation. Erskine, a Southerner by birth, came to South Bend in 1911 as treasurer for Studebaker, two years later was named vice president, and ascended to the presidency in 1915. A big, hulking, and gregarious man, if he and Rockne were not soul mates, they at the least genuinely liked and respected each other.

When Rockne took over as head football coach at Notre Dame in 1918, one of his goals was to increase the seating capacity of Cartier Field, which accommodated less than 5,000 spectators. Notre Dame was playing some of the best teams in the country—Nebraska, Penn State, Rice, and Texas—all away from South Bend.

He sent a letter to prominent businessmen in South Bend, indicating that the Notre Dame football team was a great advertisement for the city and appealed to them to purchase season tickets, thus increasing attendance and gate receipts. The Studebaker Corporation purchased 20 season tickets for the 1919 season at $5 each. Erskine's note to Rockne with the payment stated, "We at Studebaker will support every movement for the welfare and advancement of the University and in its various activities."

In January of '28 Paul Castner, an All-American fullback on Rockne's 1922 team, was the sales manager for the commercial division at Studebaker. He lobbied Studebaker vice president Paul Hoffman to sign Rockne as a motivational speaker at Studebaker's automobile conventions and dealer banquets. Rockne accepted an offer of $5,000 a year from Hoffman to be the special representative for Studebaker beginning in the winter of 1929.

The timing was ideal both for Studebaker and Rockne. For Studebaker, Rockne fit perfectly in the company's annual national sales campaign. For Rockne, it was the time between the end of the football season and the beginning of spring practice. Notre Dame president Father Charles O'Donnell had no objection to Rockne accepting the Studebaker offer.

Erskine was the chairman of the University of Notre Dame's lay board of trustees in the late 1920s. His generosity toward Notre Dame was remarkable. In 1927 Notre Dame officials announced that the university was in need of a $10 million endowment fund. Erskine gave $50,000 personally, the Studebaker Corporation contributed another $100,000, and largely through Erskine's efforts, $350,000 was raised in and around South Bend.

Rockne's first talk came in January 1929 at the National Automobile Chamber of Commerce at the Commodore Hotel in New York City. In the audience was a who's who of the automobile industry, including Henry Ford Sr. and General Motors's Alfred Sloane Jr. According to Castner, "When Rock signed off with his traditional `Go, Go, Go,' he had the entire audience, including Ford and Sloane, on their feet cheering like a bunch of college sophomores at a Yale-Harvard game."

On March 19, 1931, following his second straight national championship, Rockne signed a new contract with Studebaker for $10,000 a year to become its manager for sales promotions.

Rockne attacked his new job with his customary vigor and enthusiasm. On March 24 he addressed his first letter to the company's dealers and salesmen, titled "Carrying the Fight to the Enemy." In it, he compared aggressiveness on the football field with his desire to develop offensive-minded dealers and sales managers who would play the game in enemy territory. Six days later, on the afternoon of March 30, while in Chicago to celebrate his mother's birthday, he made a recording titled "Studebaker Champions," with the theme of turning suspects (potential car buyers) into prospects (actual car buyers). It was his last recording. The next day, Tuesday, March 31, Rockne lost his life in a tragic airplane crash in a cattle pasture near Bazaar, Kansas.

What about the Rockne automobile, the six-cylinder vehicle named after him? There are several myths surrounding this car. The most prevalent and erroneous one is that Studebaker produced the car while Rockne was still coaching. The first Rockne automobile actually went into production in December 1931, nine months after his death.

Beginning as early as 1928, Erskine felt that Studebaker needed to reenter the low-priced car market. The stock market crash of 1929 did little to dampen his enthusiasm for expansion. Following declining sales and profits in 1930, he was presented with an opportunity to do so. Willys-Overland had hired two

Rockne and Studebaker, two legendary names in South Bend, came together to market a vehicle in 1928.

Detroit engineers, Ralph Vail and Roy Cole, to design a low-priced, six-cylinder car to replace its aging Whippet. Willys liked the Vail-Cole car but lacked the capital to put it into production. The two engineers were paid for their work and were allowed to keep the two prototypes and the rights to the engineering of the car.

In the summer of 1930 Vail showed his prototype to Erskine at the Studebaker headquarters. Erskine took it for a spin, and, before the sun had set, Studebaker owned the rights to the car and hired Cole and Vail. Erskine made a full commitment to the car. He established a separate division of Studebaker, complete with its own dealer organization and engineering and production facilities in Detroit.

Following Rockne's death and with the permission of Bonnie Rockne, Erskine named the car after his beloved friend. He promised to pay Bonnie and her family 25¢ for every Rockne sold. He was confident that the magic of the Rockne name, combined with its being a fine economical vehicle, would result in a best seller.

Two models, both with four body styles, went on the market in February 1932. The Model 65 cost from $585 for a regular coupe to $740 for a deluxe convertible. The prices for the Model 75 ranged from $685 for a coupe to $780 for a deluxe sedan.

According to author Thomas Bonsell, the Rockne did far better than its brief life span and reputation would suggest. In 1932 Studebaker built about 45,000 cars and more than 23,000 were Rocknes. With the Rockne leading the way, Studebaker maintained 92 percent of its 1931 sales volume. This was at the height of the Depression, when the entire automobile industry was down 43 percent compared to its 1931 production. And the company moved up to fifth place in the automobile sales standings for 1932.

Another 15,000 were produced in 1933, bringing the total Rocknes built to just over 38,000. But that year turned out to be the darkest in Studebaker history. With its capital depleted, heavily in debt with serious cash-flow problems and unable to meet payments on its bank loans, the company was forced into receivership in March. On July 1, burdened with these problems, forced out as president of Studebaker, suffering from both a heart condition and diabetes, and in deep depression, Erskine took his own life. The Studebaker Corporation then made the decision to cease production of the Rockne automobile.

Despite the tragic deaths of Rockne and Erskine and those dark days for Studebaker in 1933, this story does have a happy ending. Under the leadership of Paul Hoffman, Studebaker rallied in the 1930s and, by the outbreak of World War II, reemerged as one of the top automakers in America. In a 10-page article in October 1946, *Life* magazine called Studebaker "the epitome of U.S. Industrial Accomplishment."

If Rockne were with us today, he would be most proud that the triumvirate of South Bend, Notre Dame, and the Studebaker Corporation (no longer manufacturing cars but now a leasing corporation) is still flourishing. In March 2005, a beautiful sculpture created by the world-renowned sculptor and Notre Dame graduate Jerry McKenna was dedicated at the College Football Hall of Fame in downtown South Bend. On the final weekend of October 2005 the sparkling new Studebaker National Museum, located just a few blocks from the College Football Hall of Fame, had its grand opening featuring Rockne memorabilia.

Knute Kenneth Rockne's legacy is now preserved forever in the heart of his hometown—South Bend, Indiana.

chapter 2
The Elmer Layden Years

Graduating cum laude in 1925, Elmer Layden helped begin a tradition of true student-athletes at Notre Dame that still permeates the program today.

Mike Layden, younger brother of coach Elmer Layden, played a prominent role in the famed 1935 Notre Dame–Ohio State clash in Columbus. He scored the second Irish touchdown as Notre Dame rebounded from a 13-0 deficit to win in what has since been selected as the greatest game in the first 100 years of intercollegiate football.

Catching Up with...Mike Layden

It is a cold mid-November day in 1924. Mike Layden trots over to the players' bench, over to Coach Rockne, who looks down at the wistful, shivering, black-haired, 11-year-old boy beside him. "What do you think of your older brother?" he asks.

"I think he's the greatest football player in the world," replies Francis Louis "Mike" Layden, a slim little kid from Davenport. "I hope I'm as good as he is when I get big."

Just 10 years after this fateful encounter, Mike Layden would move from the back story to a feature story in his own right. Instead of watching Elmer roam the gridiron as one of the Four Horsemen, Mike was now playing under "Coach Layden" as a third-string halfback. Coming off the bench to make his first collegiate start at Southern California in 1934, Layden scored Notre Dame's only two touchdowns in a 14–0 win over the Trojans to grab headlines across the nation.

Certainly, one would think Layden, now living in Indianapolis, must remember moments like these.

Knute Rockne? He called Rock a friend. The Four Horsemen? He called Elmer his brother. Game of the Century? He called it a "good day," with a performance that helped spark the legendary comeback at Ohio State in his all-star season of 1935.

But while the thought that crosses his mind will seem to be nonsense to the nonbeliever, to the Notre Dame family, it is the prevailing vocation: "There is a feeling at Notre Dame of community, where each person enjoys and likes the other and is happy," says Layden. "There is a spirit here."

In personifying this spirit, Layden's collegiate career and life afterward amazingly foreshadowed the significance of a Notre Dame student-athlete even before that term became part of campus vernacular.

Graduating cum laude in 1935 with five monograms in track-and-field and in football, Layden received the Byron V. Kanaley Award given to the graduating monogram winner deemed most commendable as a student and leader. He would later serve as president of the Notre Dame Monogram Club and take part in such community efforts as the Boy Scouts, American Red Cross, and Evansville Cancer Society.

In addition to career-long employment with Indiana Bell, Layden worked for three decades as a Big Ten official—and was booed each time his name was announced in Columbus until his retirement.

"They must have a good memory," laughs Layden.

So does the Notre Dame community.

When he returns for Irish home games, Layden walks into Notre Dame Stadium as the most exemplary living link to the structure's infancy because of the manner in which he and his brother helped build the program before and after the initial stadium bricks were laid. But a lifetime later, it is Layden's legacy off the field that built the strongest foundation of all. And for which he is most remembered.

chapter 3
The Frank Leahy Years

The dynamic Frank Leahy invoked the "alma mater clause" in his contract as coach at Boston College and left to take his dream job as head coach at Notre Dame in 1941.

Leahy produced four consensus national championships, four Heisman Trophy winners, and his Irish players who suited up in the four seasons from 1946 to 1949 never lost a game. Leahy's record from 1941 to 1949 (not counting 1944 and 1945, when Leahy was serving in World War II) was an amazing 60–3–5.

Angelo Bertelli: Pioneer of a Tradition

Pioneering is for neither the faint of heart nor the limited in ability.

Lewis and Clark had their share of life-threatening adventures during their travels out West, as did Alan Shepard, Neil Armstrong, and company during space exploration in the 1960s.

In 1942 Angelo Bertelli's setbacks as Notre Dame's original T formation quarterback weren't nearly as dramatic, but it made him a pioneer nonetheless. It also helped mold him into Notre Dame's first of seven Heisman Trophy winners, and began the school's unparalleled excellence at quarterback for the next 60-plus years. The athletic gifts of Bertelli were evident long before he won the Heisman. At Springfield (Massachusetts) Cathedral High School, Bertelli was talented enough in hockey to be wooed by the NHL's Boston Bruins and skilled enough in baseball to be courted by the St. Louis Cardinals and Detroit Tigers.

Yet it was in football where Bertelli—a.k.a. "The Springfield Rifle"—earned the most acclaim. As a resident of Massachusetts, Bertelli appeared destined to sign with burgeoning national power Boston College. Under dynamic new coach Frank Leahy, a 1931 Notre Dame graduate, Boston College finished 9–2 during Bertelli's senior year in high school—and would follow with an 11–0 mark the ensuing season. However, not even Leahy's per-suasive powers were enough to lure Bertelli away from Notre Dame. One of Bertelli's neighbors, 1940 Notre Dame captain Milt Piepul, convinced him to ink with the Irish rather than soar with the Eagles. Still, Bertelli was wistful about his decision.

"I wish coaches Leahy and [assistant Ed] McKeever were at Notre Dame instead of Boston College, not that I have anything against Boston College," Bertelli said after his signing.

In an epic moment in Notre Dame's football history, Bertelli's wish was granted during the second semester of his freshman year. Irish head coach Elmer Layden, after a successful seven-year run, resigned his post to become commissioner of the National Football League, and Leahy invoked the "alma mater clause" in his contract to take his dream job at Notre Dame in 1941.

Even Notre Dame's other Heisman Trophy–winning quarterbacks have called Angelo Bertelli the finest passer the university has ever had.

Matching Bertelli with Leahy was as propitious as linking John Huarte with first-year Notre Dame coach Ara Parseghian in 1964, uniting Tony Rice with first-year Notre Dame head coach Lou Holtz in 1986, and combining Brady Quinn with first-year Irish head coach Charlie Weis in 2005.

One provided the talent, the other the guidance, and in each case the Notre Dame football program underwent a renaissance.

In Leahy's inaugural campaign, Notre Dame finished third in the country, and Bertelli's .569 completion percentage led the nation. He also became Notre Dame's first 1,000-yard passer in a single season. In the 19 previous campaigns, no Irish player threw for more than 483 yards. No one with Bertelli's passing ability had been seen in the Midwest, and only the Sammy Baughs and Davey O'Briens from the Southwest in the 1930s were comparable.

That same year, Bertelli became the first sophomore in college football annals to finish runner-up in the Heisman Trophy balloting, with Army's Glenn Davis (1944), Georgia's Herschel Walker (1981), San Diego State's Marshall Faulk (1992), and Florida's Rex Grossman (2001) joining him in that category over the next 60 years.

It was Notre Dame's first unbeaten season in 11 years, or since Knute Rockne's 10–0 finish in 1930—yet it wasn't good enough for Leahy.

Mindful of the future, Leahy refused to stand pat with Rockne's old box formation that had Harry Wright calling the signals at quarterback and Bertelli serving as the main passer at left halfback, as well as a punter and runner.

By the late 1930s, a football revolution was emerging. Under George Halas, the NFL's Chicago Bears had implemented the T formation. The architect of the scheme, which now included the quarterback stationed behind the center, was Clark Shaughnessy, who would be named the head coach at Stanford University.

In 1940 the Bears won the NFL title with a 73–0 dismantling of the Washington Redskins. That same year, first-year Stanford coach Shaughnessy took a team that scored only 54 points during a 1–7–1 campaign in 1939 and transformed it into a unit that finished 10–0, scored 196 points, and defeated Nebraska in the Rose Bowl.

Suddenly, the T formation was all the rage, and someone with Bertelli's passing acumen fit it to a tee. In Bertelli's junior year (1942), Leahy asked for and received permission from the school's executive vice president, Rev. John J. Cavanaugh, C.S.C., to scrap Rockne's system so he could take the Notre Dame football program to a higher plane. He even hired Bears assistant Robert Snyder to help install the new scheme.

"We started almost as soon as the '41 season was over," Bertelli said. "We practiced hours and hours and hours. Every spare minute....With the man in motion and the faking, the backs were running in all directions, and the man with the ball was going into the line without interference.

"It raised some eyebrows that he didn't have all that mass blocking out in front of him. It was all brand-new to us."

Alas, new expeditions sometimes get derailed by pitfalls. Bertelli, now at quarterback instead of left halfback, struggled with the legerdemain and depth involved in the new attack, and the Irish unveiled their new offense with a 7–7 tie against Wisconsin, followed by a 13–6 loss to Georgia Tech. Bertelli had passed for only 150 yards in the two games combined and was overwhelmed by calling the signals and plays. Leahy took responsibility for the downfall, saying the extra 80 to 100 plays he gave Bertelli to study created sensory overload.

"He was very mellow until after the first game," said Bertelli of Leahy. "After the second, he went to the hospital."

Leahy was eviscerated by Notre Dame alumni for daring to repair what wasn't broken, and on the Thursday before the third game, versus Stanford, he collapsed at his desk. Leahy blamed the condition on an old back injury and other ailments, but the Irish coach was particularly suffering from the backlash of a 0–1–1 start.

Although he couldn't be at the Stanford game, Leahy had implemented a new plan of attack for Bertelli: Wright, who moved from halfback to guard, would call the signals for Bertelli, and he would also get help from halfback Pete Ashbaugh. That way, Bertelli could just concentrate on passing.

Voilá! Bertelli completed 14 of 20 passes for 233 yards and a school record four touchdowns in the 27–0 victory over the then-named Indians. He completed 10 consecutive tosses in the contest, another school standard that lasted 56 years. There were still plenty of snafus during Notre Dame's 7–2–2 season in 1942, but the bugs were worked out prior to the 1943 national title run. That year, the Irish offense was unstoppable, averaging 43.5 points per game in the six games where the runaway Heisman Trophy winner directed the attack.

Bertelli couldn't finish the campaign because of World War II obligations, but he had set the table for future Notre Dame quarterbacks to prosper. In the 11 seasons under Leahy, from 1941 to 1943 and 1946 to 1953, three other Irish quarterbacks would be enshrined in the College Football Hall of Fame: Heisman winner John Lujack, Bob Williams, and Ralph Guglielmi. A fourth, Frank Tripucka, steered the Irish to a 9-0-1 record in 1948. Still, Bertelli was the trailblazer.

"The finest passer Notre Dame ever had," said Lujack when he learned of Bertelli's death at age 78 on June 26, 1999.

"Unquestionably the best passer I've ever seen," added Tripucka, who played professionally for 15 years. "He was the blueprint for the T formation."

Bertelli left behind his wife of 54 years, Gilda, five children, and several grandchildren. After his three-year pro career was truncated by a knee injury, Bertelli ran a beverage distributorship in Clinton, New Jersey.

His impact was felt beyond just the gridiron. Bob Kelly, an All-American halfback for Notre Dame in 1944, recalled his first nervous day on campus.

"I started across the quad toward the dining hall, and this fellow came up to me and asked where I was going," Kelly began. "I told him I was going to get something to eat and he said he'd go along.

"I thought introductions were in order, so I said, 'I'm Bob Kelly.' He said, 'I'm Angelo Bertelli.' I couldn't believe it! Angelo Bertelli was escorting a 17-year-old freshman across the campus. He took me through the line and stayed with me while I ate. That's the way he was."

Indeed, Bertelli was a leader, and a pioneer, in Irish lore.

Memorable Moment: Bertelli's Final Game

Imagine an All-American quarterback today leading his team to a 6-0 record and number one ranking—and then leaving the team and school for military duty.

It was a way of life in 1943, when the United States was in the middle of World War II, and that era made Angelo Bertelli one of the more unique winners of the Heisman Trophy.

Entering his senior year in 1943, Bertelli was aware that he would be called up to join the Marine Corps on November 1. Notre Dame was on a three-semester schedule back then, and the first semester was to end October 30.

"Knowing in advance didn't make it any easier to go, though," Bertelli recalled years later.

With Bertelli at the throttle to start the 1943 season, Notre Dame asserted its dominance by outscoring its first five opponents 228–25, beginning with a 41–0 rout of Pitt on the road:

- After losing at home to Georgia Tech 13–6 the previous year, Notre Dame annihilated the Yellow Jackets in Atlanta 55–13.
- After losing to Michigan 32–20 at home in 1942, Notre Dame traveled to Ann Arbor in the third game of the 1943 campaign and manhandled the second-ranked Wolverines 35–12.
- In game four, Frank Leahy's juggernaut crushed Wisconsin 50–0, a team that tied the Irish 7–7 in the 1942 opener.
- In game five, the Illinois program that barely lost to Notre Dame in 1942 (21–14) was whipped 47–0.

The Irish were the nation's premier college team, but their on-field leader would no longer be with them after the October 30 showdown with third-rated Navy at Cleveland. The Midshipmen would finish number four in the country that year, and Notre Dame was installed as only a 10-9 favorite prior to the clash.

Working in Notre Dame's favor was an overwhelming will to "Win One for Bert."

The day before the team left for Cleveland, the *South Bend Tribune* reported: "So great is the blond Italian's [Bertelli] popularity among his teammates that the latter have literally whipped themselves into a lather over the desire to win the game for him as their final 'present' against his departure for marine corps officer training on Monday." Bertelli may have saved his best for last while playing in front of a capacity crowd of 77,900 in Municipal Stadium.

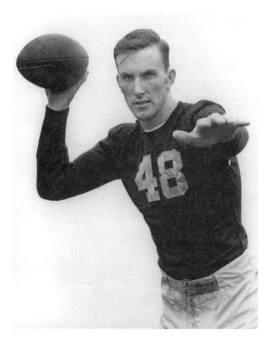

When Angelo Bertelli won the Heisman Trophy in November 1943, he couldn't attend the award ceremony at the Downtown Athletic Club in New York City because of his Marine Corps obligations.

Staking the Irish to a 13–6 halftime lead, Bertelli connected on a 49-yard touchdown pass down the sideline to Julie Rykovich and a 52-yard scoring toss across the middle to Creighton Miller. By the end of the third quarter, Bertelli tossed his third touchdown pass, to John Yonakor on fourth-and-goal from the 2, and added his third extra point after directing another touchdown drive.

In the fourth quarter Bertelli's backup, sophomore John Lujack, was inserted, but after the understudy directed the Irish to the Navy 1-yard line, Bertelli was sent in to score his final Notre Dame touchdown, earning a thunderous ovation from the overflowing crowd in the 33–6 conquest.

Bertelli finished the day five of nine, passing for 115 yards and three touchdowns, and ran for a fourth score. For the season, he was 25 of 36 (69.4 percent) for 512 yards and a Notre Dame record 10 touchdowns.

"How difficult would it be to leave for boot camp?" Bertelli was asked.

"Well, the Marines have never been beaten, either, so I figure I'm just going from one unbeaten team to another," Bertelli replied.

Although he would not play in the final four games while training in Parris Island, South Carolina, Bertelli was still the overwhelming winner of the Heisman, finishing with 648 points to runner-up Bob O'Dell's (Penn) 177. In third place was Northwestern's Otto Graham with 140.

Notre Dame lost to the semi-pro Great Lakes Seahawks on a 46-yard Hail Mary touchdown pass with 33 seconds left in the November 27 regular-season finale, but because the Irish had defeated the teams that finished second (Iowa Pre-Flight), third (Michigan), and fourth (Navy)—as well as number nine Northwestern, number 11 Army, and number 13 Georgia Tech— they were the easy pick to win the 1943 national crown.

Ironically, Notre Dame lost to Great Lakes on the same day— November 27—Bertelli received the telegram that he had won the Heisman.

"There were about five of us from Notre Dame listening to the game on the radio," Bertelli recalled. "I was just coming out of a Quonset hut after the game ended when somebody handed me a telegram telling me I'd won the Heisman. I didn't know how to feel that night."

When the Downtown Athletic Club requested Bertelli's presence in New York City for the presentation, it received a terse wire in return from his military branch: "Regret to advise you impractical to grant request for presence of Pvt. Angelo Bertelli at Downtown Athletic Club. Bertelli now undergoing training at Parris Island...any absence for even limited time materially affects his chances for selection [into officer candidates school]...in view of which it is necessary to disapprove request."

It was a different era, but Bertelli's stature as the epitome of an All-American never changed.

The Ultimate Notre Dame Player/Man

If a Mount Rushmore were to be carved one day for Notre Dame's football players, debates would rage on who the four engraved faces should be.

However, there would be two absolutes: George Gipp and John Lujack.

Gipp is immortalized in Irish lore as Notre Dame's first player to capture the nation's imagination through his life and death, while Lujack forever remains the centerpiece of Notre Dame's unparalleled era of excellence in the 1940s that included four national titles and two other unbeaten seasons.

"The two greatest winners of the 1940s were FDR and John Lujack," said the pope of college football, ESPN's Beano Cook. "But even Roosevelt won only two elections in the 1940s while Lujack won three national titles."

A product of the "Greatest Generation," Lujack, born January 4, 1925, grew up during the Great Depression, interrupted a prosperous college football career by serving in World War II from 1944 to 1945, and returned to the States to quarterback Notre Dame to national titles in 1946 and 1947, winning the Heisman Trophy in his senior year.

An avid golfer, Lujack's football skills were analogous to Jack Nicklaus's career on the links. There were some golfers who drove the ball better than Nicklaus, or putted better, or were more consistent with the mid-range game, chips and short irons...and still others who were more colorful. Yet, combine all the elements of the sport, and there was nobody from his era that rivaled Nicklaus.

So it was with Lujack. There were players in his time, including teammates, who ran better, passed with greater efficiency, hit harder, kicked more accurately, or appeared more intimidating. But combine every facet of the game—and toss in leadership and charisma for good measure—and no one possessed the complete football package the way Lujack did.

The Connellsville, Pennsylvania, native looks back in amazement at the path his career took at Notre Dame. In today's booming world of high school football recruiting ranking services and five-star ratings for the elite athletes, Lujack probably would have been a "two-star" player when he enrolled at Notre Dame in 1942.

"In my senior year of high school [1941], they named four teams all-state in Pennsylvania, and I didn't make any of the four teams," Lujack recalled.

"I did make all-county, but then my good friend and teammate Creighton Miller liked to say, 'I understand that your high school was the only one in the county.' That wasn't true, but it did make people laugh.

"Honestly, I didn't think I was good enough to get a scholarship to attend Notre Dame. I told people that if I could just make the traveling squad in my junior or senior year, I could probably come back to Connellsville, run for mayor, and win it hands down."

On Lujack's first day of practice, second-year head coach Frank Leahy asked for a freshman defensive team to scrimmage against the vaunted varsity. Notre Dame was coming off an 8–0–1 season, but Leahy was installing a new offense, the T formation, to better utilize the passing skills of junior quarterback Angelo Bertelli, the Heisman Trophy runner-up as a sophomore in 1941. The unit needed all the scrimmage work it could get, even if it meant using the freshmen as cannon fodder.

Lujack just happened to be in the front row of freshman backs when an assistant coach randomly pointed to him and a few others up front and referred to them as "you, you, you, and you" to scrimmage with the varsity.

At 165 pounds, Lujack braced himself for the worst. He was lined up at safety and told himself the only way he would survive was to "move forward" and hit with a passion.

"The quick openers with the left halfback and right halfback were coming right at me on just about every play," Lujack said. "I started making tackles, and Leahy stopped practice three different times to ask who made that tackle. The first time they had to ask my name.

"The next day when we were asked for a defensive team again, they said 'Lujack, where are you?' I raised my hand, and then they said, 'You, you, and you, go down there on defense with Lujack!' That's kind of how it all got started."

It didn't take long to recognize Lujack's skills on offense as well, and Leahy used the 17-year-old freshman in different capacities to prepare the defense. The opener that year was against Wisconsin, led by legendary Elroy "Crazy Legs" Hirsch.

"If we were going to play a T formation team, then I was the quarterback that ran the plays against the varsity," Lujack explained.

"If we were playing a single-wing team, then I would be the single-wing tailback. Sometimes I would run a simple off-tackle play and gain seven or eight yards. Leahy would go crazy at the defense and say, 'Look at this 17-year-old lad gaining eight yards against you! What do you think Elroy Hirsch is going to do? Let's run that play over again!'

John Lujack was one of the main engines powering Notre Dame's dominance in the 1940s.

"Well, now everybody knew what play was coming, the defense was steamed, everybody converges on me, and I get nailed—but I loved every minute of practice that freshman year. I just thought it was great."

Eligible for varsity action as a sophomore in 1943, Lujack was actually given the start over the senior Bertelli in the opener because it was at Pittsburgh, near Lujack's hometown. Bertelli ended up playing most of the game, but Lujack's start was a gesture of respect from the head coach.

Later that year, after directing a 6–0 start, Bertelli began basic training with the Marines on November 1 in Parris Island, South Carolina, putting Lujack behind the throttle. His first three starts came against third-rated Army, eighth-ranked Northwestern, and second-rated Iowa Pre-Flight, all Irish victories in which Lujack excelled on offense and defense to lead Leahy to his first national title.

Not even a 19–14 loss to semi-pro Great Lakes in the closing seconds of the finale was enough to sway voters to knock Notre Dame from the number one perch. That year, the Irish defeated the teams that finished second, third, fourth, ninth, 11th, and 13th in the Associated Press poll.

After the season, Lujack joined thousands of other college players in World War II duty overseas before returning in 1946 and becoming the first—and still lone—quarterback to direct three major college national titles.

While his career passing statistics .514 completion percentage, 2,080 yards, and 19 touchdowns are pedestrian by today's standards, measuring Lujack by his passing output would be like judging Bill Russell by how many points he scored during the Boston Celtics' dynasty in the 1960s, or evaluating Derek Jeter by how many home runs he hit when the New York Yankees won four World Series titles in the five years from 1996 to 2000.

Ironically, Lujack's signature play was his open-field, touchdown-saving tackle of Army's Doc Blanchard, the 1945 Heisman winner, in the 0–0 slugfest of 1946 versus the two-time defending national champs. It remains the most famous tackle in school history and helped Notre Dame achieve another national title.

"I've been asked many times, 'Were you better on defense or offense?'" Lujack said. "I didn't feel I was better in one or another, but I thoroughly enjoyed playing both ways."

During his abbreviated four-year career with the Chicago Bears, Lujack intercepted a rookie-record eight passes, threw for an NFL single-game record of 468 yards the next season, and made the Pro Bowl in his last two years.

Oh, by the way, because he also was the kicker, he led the Bears in scoring in all four of his years. What else would you expect from the last four-sport monogram winner from Notre Dame? One time in the spring of 1944, the quarterback in football and starting guard in basketball had three hits in a baseball game and, between innings, won the high jump and javelin in a track meet.

No wonder in 1951 Lujack was on the Wheaties cereal box!

Before embarking on his career as a partner in an automobile dealership business, he served as an assistant coach for Leahy's last two seasons, when the Irish finished third (1952) and second (1953) in the final AP poll. Many years later for *Sport* magazine, Lujack shared one of his favorite lessons from Leahy.

The Irish head coach was a stickler for perfection and would repeat a play in practice until it met his standards. Consequently, the same running back on a certain call would sometimes absorb a lot of punishment while repeating the play. On one occasion, a back who had a reputation for faking injuries after three or four plays repeated that act. Lujack recalled Leahy going over to this player.

"Lad, I've been watching you on every play," Leahy said, "and I realize that this bodily contact is starting to get a little bit tough because you keep getting hit. But lad, if I were to let you disassociate yourself with this scrimmage, when you're not wounded like you say you are, I would be doing you a great injustice.

"If this were to become a habit with you, then later in life when it came time to make an important business or family decision, you might also fake an injury. This we won't have from a Notre Dame man. So lad, get back in the scrimmage."

After that, Lujack said, the back had a better appreciation of what was expected of him, and he became a better man for it.

There were minimal expectations for John Lujack when he enrolled at Notre Dame in 1942. He graduated as the ultimate Notre Dame icon, and to this day he remains the model Notre Dame man.

10 Questions with John Lujack

While growing up in the 1930s in Connellsville, Pennsylvania, one of John Lujack's favorite childhood activities was listening to Notre Dame football games on the radio. On a piece of paper, he would draw the lines of a football field and chart the progress of the game.

By 1942 Lujack was suiting up for Frank Leahy's Fighting Irish en route to one of the most glamorous football careers ever. After helping lead a national title drive in 1943, he served a two-year World War II naval stint aboard a sub-chaser off the coast of England in 1944 and 1945 before returning to Notre Dame to help engineer two more national titles.

With his All-Pro career on both sides of the ball cut short by injuries, Lujack coached with Leahy for two years before going into an automobile partnership business with his father-in-law in Davenport, Iowa. Retired since 1988, Lujack has established a generous academic scholarship endowment at Notre Dame.

These days, Lujack splits his time residing in Bettendorf, Iowa, and Indian Wells, California, with his wife, Pat.

Question: What was your introduction to Notre Dame football?

John Lujack: I think the first game that I can remember listening to was the Ohio State–Notre Dame game in 1935 when I was 10 years old. We had a Philco radio that stood very high on some stilts. My head was under that radio, and when [Bill] Shakespeare threw that winning pass to Wayne Millner in the closing seconds for the 18–13 win, I was a Notre Dame fan for the rest of my life. In my senior year of high school, I remembered listening to Notre Dame–Arizona when it was Leahy's first game in his first year, and a guy by the name of Angelo Bertelli was the single-wing tailback.

It seemed to me like he completed every pass that he threw [Bertelli completed six of seven passes in the first quarter] and Bob Dove, who was an All-American end, was on the receiving end of most of them. And I said, "Boy, oh boy, that Bertelli is some kind of a player!" To be on the same team the following year in 1942 as a freshman—and to scrimmage against Bertelli and the rest of that team—it was like dreams coming true for a young kid.

Q: When Bertelli had to leave Notre Dame halfway through 1943 to join the Marines, you had to step in as a sophomore, yet you still won the national title against the country's toughest schedule. Were there any nerves on your part?

JL: I had played an awful lot in my sophomore year even before Bertelli left. Somebody had written it up that I averaged 43-and-a-half minutes per game as an 18-year-old sophomore while playing both offense and defense. I didn't come close to those kind of minutes in my junior and senior years because we were winning so decisively that other players were able to see more action. As a sophomore, I was playing both ways, I was scrimmaging against the varsity in practices…so you had enough confidence in your ability that when Bertelli—who was the best pure passer I had ever seen—left in midseason, it didn't feel like there was any added pressure. You just kind of figured, 'Let's go! Let's do the things the coach would say and let your ability take over.' Maybe I had pressure, but I was dumb enough not to recognize it. I didn't feel it at the time.

Q: What did you appreciate the most playing for coach Frank Leahy?

JL: Frank Leahy was as good a fundamentalist as any coach I've run into—and I played in Pro Bowl games, college all-star games. I've been around a lot of the great ones, but he was the best. Leahy covered all the intricacies of football, from the weakest thing to the strongest. We had a meeting one time with the quarterbacks, and his question was, "In the event that you were going to take an intentional safety in the end zone, how would you go about doing it?" We said we'd take one knee when we're just about to be hit. His answer was, "No, no, you run out of the end zone! That way no one could touch you and there would be no chance of a fumble." That's just one example of the little things that he covered daily. Any situation in a game you were involved in, he had already covered, so you never felt unsure once it was time for the game. He did the same for your business life, personal life, and spiritual life. In 1952 and 1953, after I had retired from pro football, I was the quarterbacks coach at Notre Dame, and Ralph Guglielmi and Tom Carey were the quarterbacks then. I never enjoyed two years as much as I enjoyed working with Leahy and coaching the kids at Notre Dame.

Q: *Do you think Coach Leahy's methods as a martinet would work today?*

JL: I think he would be every bit as good today as he was back then. If you're going to be a great coach, you have to have discipline, you have to have fundamentals, you have to have the players' respect, and you have to be able to teach and adjust to different things in the game. None of that changes in coaching. In Leahy's first year at Notre Dame [1941], he was undefeated. But then the next year he changed to the T formation, a complete change in Notre Dame's past philosophy. Now, when you're undefeated in your first try, how many people do you think would change things? That just shows you how he was. He recognized that the T formation was going to be the formation of the future and what happened in the past didn't matter.

Q: *Although you are recognized mainly as a quarterback, your defining play was the open-field tackle of Army's Doc Blanchard in 1946 to preserve the 0–0 tie. That eventually helped win the national title. Have you ever met Blanchard since then?*

JL: I talked to Doc Blanchard about 25 years ago, and he said to me, "Do you remember that tackle you made on me in the 1946 game?" I said, "I sure do!" And he says, "Boy, you scared the hell out of me!" So I puffed out my chest and I said, "Really, how?" He said, "I thought I had killed you." That's a made-up story, but it's a good banquet story.

Q: *So you've never met Blanchard?*

JL: No, I haven't, but I spend a lot of time in California where Blanchard's old running mate, Glenn Davis, lived. Over the course of his lifetime we played many rounds of golf together and we recalled that Army game where both offenses weren't good that day and maybe the coaches were too conservative. I think that was one of the poorest games I played. One time we were kidding over a couple of beers, and Glenn said, "That was a very lucky tackle because you caught Doc by the last shoestring." He said it was the worst tackle he had ever seen.

Q: Were there any other defining games in your career that you remember more fondly than that Army game?

JL: As an 18-year-old I played all 60 minutes against the Iowa Pre-Flight, a semi-pro team that was assembled during the war. We were ranked number one and they were number two, and we won 14–13. Perry Schwartz was an all-league end in the NFL, and I was guarding him on defense. He comes down about 12 to 14 yards and breaks out to the sideline toward the Notre Dame bench. I'm on him pretty good, but the pass is out in front of me, so I try to knock it down with one hand. Well, for some strange reason, the point of that ball stuck in the middle of my hand and resulted in a one-handed interception. Jim Costin, the sports editor at the *South Bend Tribune*, wrote that up as one of the greatest plays he's ever seen, but I think it was lucky that the ball kind of stuck in there. In pro ball, the last game of the season in 1949, my team, the Bears, are playing the Chicago Cardinals, who had the "Dream Backfield" with Elmer Angsman (also from Notre Dame), Paul Christman, Charley Trippi, and Pat Harder in the backfield. I threw six touchdown passes that day in a win and two more were downed on the 1-yard line. I had 468 yards passing—and that is still a Bears record.

Q: Who's the greatest Notre Dame player you've ever seen?

JL: There were so many good linemen. George Connor, Bill Fischer, Leon Hart, Jim Martin...but the one player who always stood out in my mind was Creighton Miller. In 1943 against Michigan in a toss-up game up there, he made two 75-yard runs, and we beat them 35–12. He led the nation in rushing that year, and no other Notre Dame back has done that. He was very fast, very tricky, and he weighed 195 pounds, which back then was quite significant.

Q: What do you think of the Heisman hype today?

JL: It's something I certainly wasn't familiar with in our day. When I was notified I won the Heisman in a telegram after the 1947 win at USC to end the season, I was the most surprised guy in the world. Winning games for Notre Dame was all that mattered to me. You can't be out for yourself. You're out for the team. If you check my records, I threw about 10 passes per game—and people do that in one quarter these days. Today a freshman or sophomore can be coming in, and a newspaperman says, "Boy, he has Heisman potential!" I think that puts a lot of pressure on a kid to perform maybe differently than he would naturally perform. If I were in the media, I would maybe write the same stuff, but it does add a lot of pressure. I remember Brady Quinn as a freshman and sophomore quarterback, he was getting killed back there because the blocking for him wasn't as good. No one was talking about him as a Heisman candidate then. But here's a guy now with passing records that I don't think will be exceeded.

Q: You were part of the golden age in Notre Dame football. In the last decade, there have been a lot of false alarms about returning to glory. The feeling is now, under Charlie Weis, the program is about to embark on another era that might not be as prosperous as Leahy's but something similar to the Ara Parseghian or Lou Holtz years.

JL: And I think Notre Dame needs that. I've always felt that the love of Notre Dame is not built necessarily around the academic standards. Now don't get me wrong, that is extremely important and I know that. But when you're talking about alumni who are 50, 60 years old, the mystique of Notre Dame is built around winning football, and that started all the way back with Rockne. You've got to win football games. If Notre Dame was to go 6–6 for the rest of our lives, don't you think that the people who grew up following and loving Notre Dame would be very disappointed, downhearted, and distressed about what has happened? Nobody wants to see a proud tradition just fade away when you grow up with that mystique and pass it on from generation to generation. I think winning football helps Notre Dame in all aspects. Under Charlie Weis, I think you will see a return to the Leahy, Parseghian, Holtz years. I think Notre Dame has made the greatest pick of anybody to coach this program.

Zygmont Always Left Them Laughing

Legendary comedian and Irish lineman Ziggy Czarobski used to shower before football practices. Finally, coach Frank Leahy asked him to explain the behavior. Said Ziggy, "It's too crowded after practice."

When the Chicago product showed up for school in 1942, he not only brought clothes, but plenty of Polish sausage and cheese, as well. "I don't know if they'll feed me right, and I'm not taking any chances."

Conversing with General Omar Bradley in a New York hotel elevator, Ziggy listened to Bradley compliment the Irish football success and then responded, "Thanks, General. And speaking for the rest of the team, we sure have enjoyed your battles."

When Leahy one day at practice decided the Irish needed a return to fundamentals, he started with a basic statement: "Gentlemen, this is a football." Ziggy's retort: "Hold it, Coach. Not so fast."

Recalled quarterback John Lujack, "Ziggy used to tell people he was in school for two terms—Roosevelt's and Truman's."

Catching Up with...Frank and Kelly Tripucka

Jersey guys are in at Notre Dame.

Current Notre Dame head football coach Charlie Weis is a Jersey guy who likes Jersey guys. Weis inherited a handful of Jersey guys and looks for a Jersey-guy mentality in players he recruits, regardless of a prospect's home state.

Tough. Quick. Nasty.

New Jersey native Frank Tripucka led the 9-0-1 1948 Notre Dame team with toughness and grit.

As Weis himself knows, Notre Dame teams at least as far back as the Frank Leahy era have had more than their share of Jersey guys.

Among the most prominent and successful was Bloomfield, New Jersey, native Frank Tripucka, a quarterback on Leahy's legendary teams of the 1940s. Tripucka earned monograms as a backup to Heisman Trophy winner Johnny Lujack on Notre Dame's unbeaten 1946 and 1947 teams before winning the starting role in 1948. He led that squad to a 9-0-1 record and a number two ranking in the final polls.

Tripucka's New Jersey influence on Notre Dame didn't end when he graduated. After becoming the first-ever starting quarterback in the history of the Denver Broncos and the first Bronco player to have his jersey retired, Tripucka and his bride and former high school sweetheart Randy settled in New Jersey. There, they raised a bunch of Jersey guys—six to be exact—with a daughter in the mix as well.

Kelly Tripucka, the fifth of those six sons, was an all-state performer in two sports in high school in Essex Fells, New Jersey. From there, Kelly followed his father's footsteps to Notre Dame, where he became an All-American...in basketball.

"I don't think Kelly likes to get hit," laughs Frank when explaining how the starting quarterback on an undefeated Irish football team could leave as his legacy to Notre Dame a basketball-playing son.

Anybody who watched Kelly Tripucka play basketball would know that Frank was joking. Without question, Kelly was a Jersey guy on the basketball court, mixing it up inside as a 6'5" forward and consistently getting under the skin of opposing players and fans alike.

Tough. Quick. Nasty.

Kelly Tripucka blended his Jersey attitude with rare talent.

As a freshman, he was a starter on Notre Dame's only men's team to reach the NCAA Final Four, while earning All-America honors in each of the next three seasons. Tripucka also infused those Irish squads with his swagger, as Notre Dame knocked off four number one teams during those four seasons, including Kentucky and Virginia on the road during Tripucka's senior season (1980–1981).

"We'd play anybody, anywhere, anytime," Tripucka says.

Tripucka, who still ranks 10th on Notre Dame's all-time scoring list, was a first-round NBA draft selection, averaging at least 20 points per game five times in a 10-year career that included two all-star game appearances.

Kelly and all of his brothers—Tracy, Mark, Todd, T.K., and Chris—began playing football in the neighborhood, in pickup games with helmets and shoulder pads.

A persistent junior high basketball coach, who also coached soccer, convinced Kelly to peel off the football gear long enough to give soccer a try.

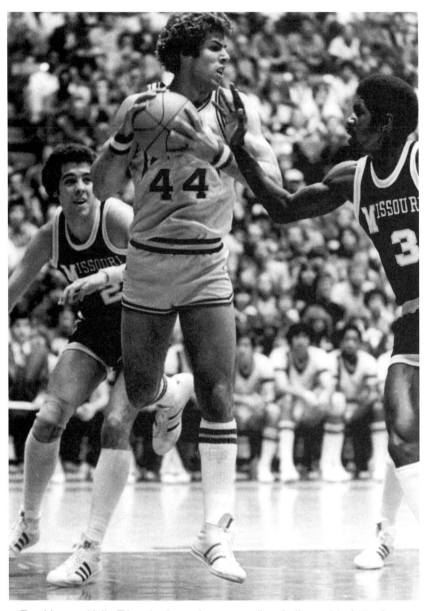

Frank's son Kelly Tripucka brought a mentality similar to his father's to the Notre Dame basketball team, where he is considered an Irish hardwood legend.

"He has a hard head," explains Frank, continuing his clinic on how to be a Jersey-guy father. "And being such a big target, he used to get most of his goals on headers."

Kelly was smart enough to use his height to his advantage when the opportunity presented, but his booming kicks are what earned Tripucka all-state honors as a sophomore and helped Bloomfield to a state soccer championship.

In spite of scholarship offers to play basketball and soccer at a number of top programs, including Duke, Maryland, and South Carolina, Kelly decided to concentrate on basketball at Notre Dame.

All six of Frank Tripucka's Jersey guys played varsity sports in college: Tracy and Todd played basketball at Lafayette; Mark played football at Massachusetts; T.K. played basketball at Fordham; and Chris, the youngest, played football at Boston College. And Heather, Tracy's twin, was a legendary competitor in several sports just as girls' sports programs were entering their infancy.

While obviously proud of the college careers of all six sons, Frank was thrilled that Kelly got a chance to play for Notre Dame, regardless of which sport.

"I could care less what sport it was," says Frank Tripucka, in the same usage favored by Jersey guy Weis (disdaining the preference of grammarians—"couldn't care less"). "I wanted all my boys to play sports. That was a strict rule—there was not gonna be anybody hanging around the house."

As father and son reminisce and laugh, Kelly rattles off dozens of his siblings' accomplishments, never mentioning his many Notre Dame and NBA records. Only a Google search revealed that Kelly was named the *Newark Star-Ledger* New Jersey High School Basketball Player of the 20th Century, and that he was inducted into the Sports Hall of Fame of New Jersey. In 2005 Kelly joined the New York Knicks, headed by former NBA teammate Isiah Thomas, as a member of the scouting staff.

You Gotta Have Hart

Only the eternally unbeaten Father Time could defeat Leon Hart.

On September 24, 2002, the 73-year-old Notre Dame icon succumbed to an illness at St. Joseph Medical Center in South Bend, just a mile from his beloved Notre Dame campus.

Only through death did Hart finally seem mortal. His biography reads that he never lost a football game in high school, and even a casual fan is probably aware he never lost while playing for Frank Leahy at Notre Dame, from 1946 to 1949. As for his pro career, it ended with the 1957 NFL title while playing with the Detroit Lions—the last time the Lions were champions (Hart also starred for the 1952 and 1953 NFL champs).

Born on November 2, 1928, in the Pittsburgh suburb of Turtle Creek, Pennsylvania, Hart became one of the most prized football prospects in the country at Turtle Creek High School. Notre Dame assistant coach and future athletics director Edward "Moose" Krause (1949–1981) could attest to Hart's value.

One spring night in 1946, while Krause was ailing in his home with an illness bordering on pneumonia, his phone rang after midnight. Krause's wife, Elise, answered, and he overheard her say that her husband was too impaired to talk.

"Who is it?" Krause grumbled from the bed, as recorded in Jason Kelly's 2002 book *Mr. Notre Dame*.

"I think his name is Leon Hart," Elise replied. "He says he's at the South Bend train station."

Apparently, a clumsily arranged recruiting trip through a Notre Dame alumnus led to Hart arriving at a late hour and with no blueprint on where to go. Hart went through the phone book to find Krause, the assistant who had been corresponding with him.

Upon hearing who the caller was, Krause jumped out of bed, grabbed the phone, told Hart in a barely audible whisper to sit tight, and then pulled a topcoat over his pajamas.

"Where are you going?" Elise demanded.

"To the train station."

"You'll die out there!"

"It doesn't matter. If I don't get Hart on the team, Frank will kill me anyway."

Despite the unconventional recruiting visit—including sleeping on a cot inside Notre Dame Stadium and having to find the football office in Breen-Phillips Hall himself the next morning—Hart became smitten with the campus and emerged as the centerpiece of the most dominant four-year era in Notre Dame football history. During Hart's four seasons, Leahy's squads posted a 36–0–2 record while winning national titles in 1946, 1947, and 1949, and finishing second in 1948.

In its end-of-the-20th-century sports recap, *Sports Illustrated* recognized Notre Dame's four-year stretch as the second-best dynasty in any sport, behind only the Boston Celtics' 11 NBA championships in 13 seasons, from 1957 to 1969.

As a senior in 1949, Hart became the last lineman in college football annals to win the Heisman Trophy. Yet his brute force and strength were complemented by athletic skills that allowed him to catch 49 career passes for a 15.5-yard average, as well as line up at fullback on occasion.

Even when he was a couple of months shy of celebrating his 18th birthday in 1946, Hart's overwhelming size and athletic skills made him a Goliath figure on a Notre Dame roster that would produce more than 40 NFL players.

"He was a big freshman; he weighed about 260 pounds," recalled teammate John Lujack, the winner of the 1947 Heisman, in an interview with the *Pittsburgh Post-Gazette*. "We tried to fool him on a couple of plays and he wasn't very 'foolable.' We knew he was going to be a great player.

"He was second team to Jack Zilly, our regular right end, and he played an awful lot as a freshman. That didn't happen a lot at Notre Dame."

Hart stepped in as the full-time starter in 1947 and was part of the most decorated line in college football history, featuring five members of the College Football Hall of Fame: consensus All-America Jim Martin (left end), 1946 Outland Trophy winner George Connor (left tackle), 1948 Outland Trophy winner Bill "Moose"

Defensive end and cocaptain Leon Hart holds the Heisman Trophy in New York City on December 7, 1949. Photo courtesy of AP/Wide World Photos.

Fischer (left guard), consensus All-American Ziggy Czarobski (right tackle), and Hart (right end).

"He was always a very dominant player, but he was also humble in that he was a strong promoter and advocate of the recognition of his teammates," Fischer remembered. "In later years, he was on the board for the Hall of Fame and fought hard for teammates such as Jim Martin and [quarterback] Bob Williams to be recognized and inducted."

Yet, football didn't consume Hart's life. It was more of an avocation, a balance to his intellectual, spiritual, and social pursuits. Much to Leahy's chagrin, Hart even had to report late to practice a couple of times each week while taking some late-afternoon engineering classes. Coaches, especially a martinet such as Leahy, often have a "no practice, no play" policy—but an exception could be made in Hart's case.

When asked where he was and what he was doing when informed that he won the Heisman, Hart, who received his degree from the College of Engineering, had an atypical response.

"What do you usually do at Notre Dame when you are not practicing football? You're studying, of course," Hart said in a 1987 interview. "I was in my room in Walsh Hall, getting ready for an examination in engineering. I received a telegram and later I had to ask my coach, John Druze, what the Heisman Trophy was."

Upon his graduation, Hart was elected as class president by his peers, which included the planning of future reunions and even setting up a "dire need fund" for classmates who may have fallen on hard times.

Although he lined up at fullback on occasion, particularly during his senior year, it was Hart's dominance in the trenches that earned him veneration nationwide. His intellectual prowess also was well known among teammates—and sometimes resented in the pros.

"Leon was always a class guy and a solid citizen, but if you were involved in an argument, he was the guy to have on your side," Fischer said.

"Leon was probably a little more intelligent than the average football player," said Hall of Fame lineman Lou Creekmur, a Detroit Lions teammate of Hart's for eight years. "He had a degree in engineering and he had an IQ that was a lot higher than the rest of us. Sometimes he'd flaunt it."

While playing for the Detroit Lions from 1950 to 1957, Hart—who also headed up a variety of business enterprises—was asked what he did in the off-season.

His response: "In the off-season, I play football."

Hart remained in the Detroit area after retiring from his off-season work, eventually becoming the founder and president of Leon Hart Industries, which produced a variety of products used by the commercial trucking industry. And just to show that football did matter to him, particularly at Notre Dame, he created a four-part video series titled "The Golden Years of Notre Dame Football, 1946–49."

Hart's wife, the former Lois Newyahr whom he married in 1950, died in 1998. The couple was survived by their six children—four of them Notre Dame graduates—and 14 grandchildren. One of Hart's progeny, Kevin, was a tight end on the 1977 national champs, and Kevin's son, Brendan, was a walk-on tight end for the Irish. The impact of the school remained everlasting and continues to perpetuate in his family.

"Notre Dame not only taught me how to make a living, but how to live," said Hart, who was buried on the Notre Dame campus next to his wife.

That experience ultimately proved to be his greatest victory during an unbeatable career.

10 Questions with Kevin Hart

When Leon Hart's son, Kevin, signed a football scholarship to play at Notre Dame in 1975, he was asked in a questionnaire if he had any past ties with the school. Hart wrote that his father participated in football at the school.

Yes, and Beethoven practiced piano, William Shakespeare did a little writing, and Jonas Salk dabbled in some medicine.

The younger Hart also won a national title while at Notre Dame, in 1977, even catching the final touchdown in the memorable 49–19 victory over USC in the green jersey game while backing up All-American tight end Ken MacAfee. He recalls his favorite memories of his father, the 1949 Heisman Trophy winner and a unanimous choice on any college football all-century team from 1900 to 1999.

Question: Why did you write down that your father merely played football at Notre Dame rather than point out that he won the Heisman?

Kevin Hart: He was sensitive to not wanting to overshadow his kids, so he never really talked about his football career that much with us. I knew the award he won was pretty special, but to me he was first a great father, not a Heisman Trophy winner. I had three older brothers who also were very good athletes, so by the time I enrolled at Notre Dame, the knowledge of my dad's football career here also was a little on the downswing.

Q: So you didn't grow up hearing too much about his exploits?

KH: He didn't volunteer it on his own, but when you could pull it out of him, it was fun. I didn't really know as much about it until after I graduated. He graduated in 1950 and I graduated in 1980, so we were always able to go together to the class reunions at Notre Dame every five years. Once he was together with the guys he went to school with, the stories came out a little more. I would go back feeling good about being on the 1977 national champs, but his group pointed out we had a loss that year. The guys he was with never lost in four years, so we felt like we were bums compared to them.

Q: Was he uncomfortable being identified as mainly a Heisman Trophy winner?

KH: He took great pride in it, but he was subtle in how he presented himself. At his funeral, one of the things that stood out to me was there were so many people who didn't even know about his football career, and that was a testament to how he lived.

Q: You didn't even have the Heisman in your home, right?

KH: No. These days, the Heisman committee presents two trophies: one to the winner and one to his school. In his time, the trophy was given only to the player—and he immediately donated his to the school.

Q: When did you develop an appreciation of your father being a Heisman Trophy winner?

KH: When I got to Notre Dame, I discovered how unbelievably difficult it is to be a student-athlete and truly came to appreciate the level he played at. Plus, he majored in engineering, and back then in road trips they would take trains that would take several days to get to where they were going, and he would have to miss classes. I enrolled in and graduated from the architecture school, and his career inspired me to believe that if he could get through engineering and play at the level he did in his era, then I could handle architecture.

Q: He had a reputation of never being shy to voice his opinion, popular or not, on certain matters. Would that be accurate?

KH: He never had trouble sleeping because he thought he didn't say the right thing. He prided himself on honesty, integrity, and directness. Some admired it, and some didn't like it. Sometimes you hear people say how someone has different personalities, being one way at work and another way around family or others. He was the same person wherever he was. He lived by a principle of being true to yourself, your family, and God.

Q: What did he appreciate the most during his time at Notre Dame?

KH: His favorite memories were going to the Grotto before a game and living among the students rather than being segregated as athletes. A lot of his best friends were fellow students, not just football players. What he always loved was the bond between the students and the team, even when I played and right to this day. I've met a lot of players from other schools, and they've said there was not that kind of affection between the regular students and the athletes. One of Dad's best friends was Jim Carberry, a roommate who became a chemical engineering professor at Notre Dame. Jim would tell him that without his football knowledge—he would do some interhall coaching—Dad wouldn't have won the Heisman. Then my dad would say, "Yeah, but I was the one who got you through freshman chemistry!" They were like a Mutt and Jeff combination.

Q: He enrolled in 1946 as a 17-year-old freshman right after World War II. Did he ever talk about assimilating with the players who had just come back from the war?

KH: He had great admiration and respect for them. He used to laugh about Jim Martin, whom he played with all four years, but Jim was about five years older than him when he returned from World War II. Jim was a war hero who would do reconnaissance missions swimming past mines, and he'd have nothing but swim goggles and a bowie knife. Then when he enrolled at Notre Dame in 1946, the policy was lights out by 10:00 or so. Here's someone who fought on three continents, an adult man, a decorated marine being given these restrictions. Dad would ask him, "How can you stand all these rules?" Jim said, "Leon, this is a piece of cake compared to what I've been through."

Q: During his pro career he was listed around 280 pounds, yet he played mainly fullback in the latter stages with the Detroit Lions. Was he the original Refrigerator Perry?

KH: People said he was like an Earl Campbell of his time because he was such a big man but still so athletic. He had good hand-eye coordination, played baseball, was a very good squash player, which is tougher than racquetball. He played basketball against us when we were growing up, and was an avid snow-skier and water-skier. He was like a big kid.

Q: The devotion of Notre Dame graduates from that era is powerful, and your father also became president of the school's Monogram Club and is buried on the campus. Did his love for Notre Dame grow with time?

KH: In his last years he would just drive down [from the Detroit area] to wander around the campus, walk into any building, and just strike up a conversation with anyone there. He sometimes wouldn't have a ticket for a game, but he would be allowed to go anywhere he wanted—the press box, the locker room...there were no boundaries from the university with him. In his final days, I think he knew what was happening to him, and you could see he just couldn't wait to get back on the campus again. We had a service for him in Michigan and then a private one at Notre Dame. When Father [Ted] Hesburgh and Father [Edmund] Joyce heard about it, they dropped everything to do the service.

Pulling Double Duty

In 1951 Leon Hart was named an All-Pro as both an offensive end and defensive end. Later, he also would line up more often at fullback.

Hart was a T-Rex of his era, but now he would just be considered another football dinosaur.

Comparing football players from different eras is an exercise in frustration. On one hand, the athletes today are much bigger, faster, and stronger than yesteryear. But to his dying day, the often outspoken Hart contended that the speed of today's game doesn't necessarily make the athletes better football players.

While many might mock that the players from the 1940s and 1950s couldn't come close to competing in today's NFL, Hart contended that another question that could be posed is whether the players from today's game could do what the athletes from his era did.

According to Hart, an athlete is defined by three attributes: ability, effort, and stamina.

"It was always Frank Leahy's contention that to win consistently, you always had to be in better shape than your opponent," Hart said in a 1989 interview.

Never mind that football eventually went to a two-platoon system where players lined up separately on offense or defense. It became even more specialized in the last two decades, where players would be specifically inserted for third-down situations or the like. Football became so specialized and strived to be perfect by the 1980s that Hart began to refer to the NFL as the National Push, Shove, Pass, Catch League. Basketball requires an athlete to play on offense and defense, and so does baseball (outside of designated hitters)…so why not football?

According to Hart, football became more specialized to reduce mistakes—but what was sacrificed were two of the three main athletic ingredients: effort and stamina.

"There are so many substitutions and specialization—in the pro game in particular—that they've removed the stamina aspect," Hart explained. "They're working for a game of no mistakes and in so doing, they've removed the stamina from the game.

"In trying to minimize the mistakes, they've taken the effort away, too. The third aspect of an athletic contest is ability, which isn't worth anything without the stamina and effort.

"Football is a team sport, and I believe they should play it the way they used to. If you leave a game in a particular quarter, you cannot go back into the game until the next quarter."

Whether you agreed or disagreed with him, Hart was not one to be reticent about his opinions.

Catching Up with...Jerry Groom

Notre Dame's "Iron Man" center has saved the Irish from utter rout. Averaged 55 minutes per game. Plays best under pressure and is an uncanny pass snatcher. Captain of the team and inspiration to mates. A senior, he's majoring in business and plans to work for his father after a year or two in pro football. —The 1950 News All-America Release

In describing its selection of Jerry Groom to the 1950 News All-America team, only the most clairvoyant sportswriter could have used proper diction to encapsulate Groom's impact on the gridiron in the decade following World War II—or begin to predict Groom's influence away from the field 50 years later.

The year or two in professional football became five with the Chicago Cardinals, including a Pro Bowl season in 1954. Plans to work for his father never fully materialized, but Groom did broadcast for the Denver Broncos before serving as a vice president with Levi Strauss & Co. and retiring with his wife Kathy in Sarasota, Florida. And in these retirement years he would continue to feel the aches and pains of his playing days. Groom has endured 14 football-related operations and boasts a pair of artificial hips and surgically repaired knees as proof.

But the most glaring omission from the passage is not that, five decades later, his efforts at Notre Dame were recognized with induction into the College Football Hall of Fame. Rather, the oversight is obvious to those who know Groom best—he was and is one of Leahy's Lads.

"Playing and graduating from Notre Dame always will be a tremendous part of my life," said Groom. "But no one has had a bigger impact than Coach Leahy."

The group of Leahy's former players has returned to campus at least once per season since its first reunion in the 1950s. But through his efforts, Groom ensures that Leahy's influence is experienced by Notre Dame students each day of the year.

In 1996 Groom helped launch the scholarship fund that bears Leahy's name with Jack Connor, John Lattner, Jack Leahy, and

Buddy Romano. Today the Frank Leahy Memorial Fund has raised more than $2 million in academic scholarships for students in need of financial assistance. Groom works tirelessly to raise donations and organize the group's annual dinner and gala.

"Ironic," says Groom. "The year I was captain was the worst record Coach ever had, at Boston College or Notre Dame."

But Leahy's relationship with Groom extended well beyond wins and losses. Just ask Groom, ever the conversationalist, and he will be glad to narrate an anecdote about his coach.

"Jerry is a phenomenal man," said Jack Leahy, sporting a twinkle in his eye eerily similar to his father's. "He keeps this thing going."

In 55 words or less, a sportswriter can only communicate so much. It sometimes takes 50 years more to tell the rest of the story.

From Cruiser to Aircraft Carrier: John Lattner

During his years at Notre Dame from 1950 to 1954, multipurpose extraordinaire John Lattner was enrolled in the Air Force ROTC.

Early in his freshman year in 1950, though, Lattner was informed by head coach Frank Leahy that he should be in another branch of the military. "Ah, Johnny Lattner, you should have been in the navy—you're a cruiser!" Leahy would tell him.

The greatest athletes have a tendency to look as if they're in cruise control, but Leahy's statement was about maximizing Lattner's skills with a more passionate effort.

"He used that line quite a bit, especially when I was a freshman," said Lattner, whose Leahy impersonations could be a road show. "I wasn't a real fast back. I was a big back for those days, about 195 pounds and close to 6'3"...but I thought I was better than a cruiser. I thought I'd be a PT boat, at least.

"My speed wasn't the best, but most of the time it was because I had no intensity. I had to push myself all the time—and Leahy would help. I had some talent, don't get me wrong, but I had to keep improving on what I had. I wasn't gifted with a lot of speed.

I could play defense and I had a little strength behind my running…but if I didn't hit the hole fast enough, or would get tackled from behind, then there was that reaction from Coach that I wasn't extending myself."

Of course, the autumn of 1950 was not a pleasant time for Leahy, who had already produced four national titles at Notre Dame and never lost a game from 1946 to 1949. But the recruiting gravy train ended in the late 1940s, injuries arose, and all of a sudden the Irish finished 4–4–1 in 1950. A product of Chicago's Fenwick High School, Lattner was the rock upon whom Leahy would return Notre Dame to glory. The Irish head coach assembled excellent recruiting classes in 1950 and 1951 that would propel three consecutive top-four finishes from 1952 to 1954, with Lattner, a two-time consensus All-American and the 1953 Heisman Trophy winner, serving as the crown jewel.

Lattner averaged an astonishing 18 yards per carry as a senior at Fenwick, but due to NCAA freshman ineligibility back then, he couldn't join the Notre Dame varsity until 1951. With the United States embroiled in the Korean War at the time, freshmen were

While he wasn't the fleetest of foot, John Lattner was the consummate all-around big-game player for the Irish in the early 1950s.

made eligible in 1951, and the genesis of one of the great back-fields in Notre Dame annals was born.

- Freshman quarterback Ralph Guglielmi started in the 19–12 victory at USC to conclude the 1951 rebuilding year (7–2–1 record), would be the fourth pick in the 1955 NFL draft, and is enshrined in the College Football Hall of Fame.
- Sophomore fullback Neil Worden, Lattner's classmate, would be the ninth pick in the 1954 NFL draft and actually finished with more yards rushing at Notre Dame (2,039) and more touchdowns (29) than Lattner (1,724 and 20, respectively).
- Freshman Joe Heap, a three-time Academic All-American, was the eighth pick in the 1955 NFL draft and became the first Irish player to eclipse 1,000 yards receiving and 1,000 yards rushing in his career. The only other player to do so since then is Raghib "Rocket" Ismail.
- Yet Lattner, the seventh pick in the 1954 NFL draft, was the centerpiece. He wasn't as swift as Heap, as powerful as Worden, or as bold as Guglielmi, but there wasn't a better all-around player in the nation, never mind at Notre Dame, during his college career.

These days, a triple-threat player is defined as a runner, receiver, and return man. In Lattner's day, it was about playing offense, defense, and special teams.

In 1952, the year Notre Dame defeated four different conference champions or cochamps—Texas, Oklahoma, Purdue, and USC—and tied Ivy League champion Penn, Lattner was the lone Irish player to start on both offense and defense. Plus, he was the punter and return man.

One year later, as a senior, Lattner didn't lead the unbeaten Irish (9–0–1) in rushing, receiving, interceptions, tackles, or touchdowns, but he still won the Heisman for his body of work.

A demon on defense, Lattner set the career interceptions record (13) at Notre Dame, could run inside or outside on offense, completed four passes for 111 yards, averaged nearly 16 yards per catch during his career, returned two of the eight kicks booted to him as a senior for touchdowns, averaged about 11 yards per punt return during his career, and handled the punting.

Like John Lujack before him and Paul Hornung after him, Lattner was the consummate "triple threat"—and then some.

He also had a propensity for playing his best when the stage was the brightest. In the 1953 opener at Oklahoma his interception sealed a 28–21 Irish victory—the last time the Sooners would lose until four years later, also to Notre Dame. In a hard-fought 28–20 win at Penn, Lattner returned a kickoff for a 92-yard score to tie the game. At archrival USC he carried 17 times for 157 yards and four touchdowns.

In between, he scored the clinching touchdown in a 27–14 win over Georgia Tech to end the Yellow Jackets' 31-game unbeaten streak. Against teams from every corner of the country, Lattner thrived—and that's how he won what remains the second-closest Heisman race in history.

"I actually lost the Midwest to [runner up] Paul Giel of Minnesota," Lattner said. "I won the East Coast vote because I had a good game against Pennsylvania, and I won the West Coast because I scored four touchdowns against Southern Cal. Television really wasn't a big impact back then. The publicity had to come from playing in areas where you could get the media's attention from all over the country."

Alas, because of a controversial 14–14 tie with Iowa, the Irish finished number two in 1953 to unbeaten Maryland. The Terrapins lost to Oklahoma—where the Irish won in the opener—in the Orange Bowl, but back then the final polls were completed after the regular season. "You sucked it up a little bit because there wasn't anything you could do about it," Lattner said. "There were five polls back then, and we won three of them, but the only two that counted were the UP and AP."

After he graduated, Lattner played with the Pittsburgh Steelers and finished third in the Rookie of the Year balloting. However, because of his ROTC commitment, he had to be with the air force the next two years, where he suffered a football career–ending knee injury while playing at one of the bases.

He might have been a cruiser early in his career, but John Lattner ultimately became the aircraft carrier for Notre Dame's football program in the early 1950s.

10 Questions with John Lattner

Ask lifetime Chicago native and resident John Lattner about his greatest achievement and he'll point to eight children and 25 grand-children for him and his wife, Peggy. But there were other memorable days at Notre Dame as well for the typically amiable Lattner.

Question: How did your introduction to Notre Dame occur?

John Lattner: I was taught by the Sisters of Mercy nuns in Chicago. Where we lived, on the West Side, there were a lot of Notre Dame people. At the time, I don't think I even knew how to walk, but I already knew Notre Dame was the epitome. I had 90 scholarship offers, but this was 1950, when Notre Dame had just completed a fourth straight unbeaten season. People were saying, "Don't go to Notre Dame because you'll just be a number there. You won't be able to play, you're not fast enough." Just a lot of negatives, particularly from the coaches who were trying to recruit me for their schools.

I knew that at least 40,000 people would come from Chicago to see a Notre Dame game because this was before television had become big. So I'd be playing in front of my home crowd. It was an added incentive for me to at least try to make the team.

Q: So here you are on the freshman team at Notre Dame, and the varsity finishes 4–4–1 in 1950—which was more losses than the three that Frank Leahy had in his first seven seasons at Notre Dame. How rough must that have been?

JL: Put it this way—we started spring practice for 1951 on December 9, 1950. We had lost a lot of personnel from those teams in the 1940s and lost a lot of people to injuries in the 1950 season. We were practicing from December 9 through December 19, until they let us go home for Christmas. When we came back after Christmas break, we used to have final exams at the end of January, so we didn't have any practice for about three weeks. Then we came back in February to practice in the fieldhouse and in the old navy drill hall. We practiced there until May 14 for the Old-Timers game.

Q: Any other stories on how obsessed Frank Leahy was with winning and getting Notre Dame back to the top?

JL: My dad died in April of my freshman year and was buried in Evansville, Indiana, where he was from. We came out of the church with the casket, and Coach was there with the assistants, Bernie Crimmins, Bill Earley, Bob McBride. Coach came up to me and said, "John, I'm awfully sorry about your father…do you have any way back to school?" He wanted me to make it back there for practice. He didn't miss a cue. We practiced a lot that spring. It paid off because we were a real young team but improved a lot the next year.

Q: You had a memorable birthday in your senior year [1953] when you ended Georgia Tech's 31-game winning streak but also saw Leahy collapse on that same day outside the locker room and nearly die. The word was you thought he was faking it. Is that accurate?

JL: My good friend from high school was Bobby Rigali. His dad, Joe, played for Rockne and he was on the national title team with the Four Horsemen. He used to tell us about some of Rockne's halftime stories. Bobby would scrimmage and was a tough kid, but because he didn't play, he was a little disgusted with Leahy. So we were sitting next to each other in the locker room at halftime and we saw Father Hesburgh go into the training room where Leahy was, Father Joyce, trainer Gene Paszkiet, and Don Penza, our captain, so we knew something was going on. Anyway, Penza comes out and he was crying and said, "The coach is dying, he's dying!" Rigali gives me a nudge and says, "Don't believe him. He's pulling a Rockne."

Q: The score was tied in the second half, and even though you found out that Leahy was in serious condition, how did you find the resolve to win?

JL: It's something that Leahy taught us to fight through. You have to concentrate completely on the game and move forward. If

John Lattner, winner of the 1953 Heisman Trophy and second-time winner of the Maxwell Trophy, receives congratulations from teammates at practice in South Bend on December 11, 1953. The players, from left, are Joe Heap, left halfback; Ralph Guglielmi, quarterback; Lattner, right halfback; Don Penza, right end and captain; and Neil Worden, fullback. Photo courtesy of AP/Wide World Photos.

you think about your mistakes, you're going to make more mistakes. We knew he was sick, but we still had to go on and beat a really good team. There were no thoughts of how bad off he was because that's how he wanted us thinking.

Q: How did you find out you won the Heisman and what do you remember the most about it?

JL: [Athletics director] Moose Krause called me, and that's how I found out. He said, "We're going to New York and you can invite your best girlfriend!" Well, I wasn't dating my wife at the time, so I took my mother. It was a wonderful experience for her. She had never flown and never been in New York. The night before the presentation, they took us for a night out on the town, and at 2:00 AM my mother and I ended up in the Copacabana in Times Square. My mother loved her martinis, and one of the people with us said, "Johnny, tomorrow's going to be a long day. We better be heading back." I said, "Well, go talk to my mother." So he explains to her that tomorrow will be a busy day and she says, "Oh, okay, instead of a martini I'll have a Miller High Life then." We stayed until 3:00 AM. She just enjoyed the dancing and was going to have a good time.

Q: *Although you didn't have a girlfriend to take to the Heisman dinner, you did spend some time with Marilyn Monroe when the team went to play USC in Los Angeles during your sophomore year [1951], correct? Can you relay the experience?*

JL: There was a film called *Clash by Night* she was doing at the time at a Los Angeles studio, so after practice about five us went over to the studio unannounced. We didn't have carte blanche to go there, but Bobby Joseph, our extra-point kicker, could talk like a million dollars. He talked his way into us getting on the set. Marilyn wasn't doing anything that morning, so we went back to practice at one of the big hotel dining hall rooms and afterward we went back to the studio and sat with her in her star hut for at least an hour. We told her we'd get her a field pass, so then she brought out her publicity pictures for us. She said, "What should I put on it?" I said, "Dear John, thank you for the wonderful night we had together. Love and kisses, Marilyn." She signed it just like that and put her phone number on it.

Later we called her up that night and said, "Marilyn, we're all set with the field pass!" She said, "John, I'd love to go but I have to pick up another athlete at the airport." You know who the other athlete was? Joe DiMaggio.

She drove us back to our hotel from the studio. There were five of us in that little car, but we had a ball. She was so delight-ful. I had a buddy in the Marine Corps who was waiting for me at the hotel. She then drove him back to the main base. What a gal!

Q: *What happened to the photo?*

JL: I lost it in a flood in the basement back in Chicago. I didn't have it up on the wall, but I should have. We had a flood that went over where I had it stored. It was no big deal. I had it hanging on my dorm wall in Morrissey Hall, but the rector made me take it down. He kept it and said, "You can get it back when you leave this dorm." So at the end of my sophomore year I got the picture back. Things were more strict back then, but at least he didn't kick me out of the dorm.

Q: *Who's the greatest Notre Dame player you've ever seen?*

JL: I never saw Angelo Bertelli play, but I loved him as a man. John Lujack was a fantastic defensive and offensive player. And Paul Hornung...Paul was a freshman when I was a senior, but you could see even then what a special talent he was. I'd be a punter for the varsity, and he'd come down from the freshman team and kick with me, and I'd say, "Paul, go back to the freshman team, you're making me look bad here!" What struck you about him was that he was so really big for those days, about 220 pounds, but so athletic.

He also had a car when he was a freshman, and I didn't as a senior. I was supposed to be like a big brother and watch over him, so before school started, I said to him one time, "Let's go to a movie!" He didn't want to and took me to Mishawaka and some bars I never heard of. We had only a couple of beers, but after a couple of days with him, I said, "Paul, if I stay with you, I won't make the team."

Q: *You've always been known as very down to earth and humble. Where did that come from?*

JL: I never expected anything. My ambition in high school was to maybe get a scholarship to a small school like Loras College or St. Benedict. To get a chance to go to Notre Dame...I didn't think I had all this in me, to be frank. I'm surprised I've had all these accolades thrown this way.

Fumble Recovery

Most Heisman Trophy winners usually have a defining game or play. For Notre Dame's Tim Brown, it was his back-to-back punt returns for touchdowns against Michigan State in 1987. For Boston College quarterback Doug Flutie, it was the Hail Mary pass at Miami in 1984. Yet, for 1953 Notre Dame Heisman Trophy winner John Lattner, maybe the most talked about game in his career is the one at Purdue in 1952, his junior year. That was the game where Lattner fumbled five times—yet, he doesn't mind rehashing the details.

"It's the only record I have left at Notre Dame," laughs Lattner. The game has become somewhat of an urban legend around campus, but some fiction also has been involved.

Fiction: Lujack's fumbles cost the Irish the game. In fact, the unranked Irish upset ninth-ranked Purdue 26–14 at West Lafayette.

In one of the most bizarre games Notre Dame ever played in, the Irish fumbled a school-record 10 times, but Purdue coughed up the ball 11 times. Notre Dame ended up recovering 15 of those 21 miscues, including a touchdown by Irish right tackle Joe Bush on a Lattner fumble in the end zone.

In that same game Lattner snared a 47-yard touchdown pass from Ralph Guglielmi on the last play of the first half to give the Irish a 20–7 lead. Even after a solid victory against a top 10 foe, though, Lattner may have made his best move once he got off the field.

"I didn't go back on the train with the team because I figured Coach Leahy was going to throw me off of it," Lattner said. "My brother drove me back to Chicago, but that wasn't too unusual because if we had a game nearby, we'd drive back to Chicago for the weekend and report for classes on Monday."

In the team meeting that Monday Leahy talked to the team about a certain back who was "a traitor to Our Lady's school because of five fumbles."

"I was ready to take off like a bandit after the meeting when I heard Leahy say, 'Ah, Mr. Lattner, I'd like to have a little chat with you.' He said, 'John, I have not been able to prepare for the upcoming game because of your fumblitis. Why would a boy of your caliber fumble five times?' I told him I couldn't explain it.

"He said, 'Ah, John, back in Chicago, do you have any girl problems that would cause you to fumble five times?'"

That wasn't it.

"Then he said, 'When you were in Fenwick High School in Chicago, did you ever go to the racetrack with your dad?' He must have known I did because I did like to play the horses with my dad on Saturday mornings.

"When I said I did place an occasion bet, he said, 'John, last Saturday, did you have a wager with the bookies on the West Side?' He thought I was betting on losing, but we ended up winning by a pretty decent margin against a team ranked ahead of us."

Satisfied that the problems weren't mental or a lack of scruples, Leahy handed Lattner a football and ordered him to carry it with him at all times.

"He said, 'If I see you around campus without this football, you'll lose your scholarship here at Notre Dame,'" Lattner said. "One of my teammates put a handle on the football to make it a little easier to carry around. I did that for a whole week. I went to classes with it, slept with it…I did everything he wanted me to do. I didn't get a lot of snickers from the fellow students, but the professors thought it was pretty cute.

"I carried it all week because I truly thought I might lose my scholarship. Leahy was a man of his word. I just put my hand on the handle and carried my books."

Fiction: It didn't solve all the fumbling problems (the Irish lost a record seven fumbles in a 21–3 loss later that year to Michigan State), but eventually the fundamentals improved.

"I might have fumbled once my senior year," Lattner recalled.

Fact: To err is human. To get a handle on it and still become the nation's most esteemed football player is divine.

Golden Memories: The 1953 Notre Dame Team

Over the years, many teams have been held up as examples of a well-coached football team. But few teams have seen their adherence to coaching have as dramatic an impact on their season as did Notre Dame's 1953 team.

Head coach Frank Leahy's final Notre Dame team began the season ranked first in the country. The Irish defeated four ranked teams in their first five games, and were 7–0 still atop the polls by the time Forest Evashevski brought his 20th-ranked Iowa Hawkeyes to Notre Dame Stadium on November 21.

Notre Dame's offense sputtered throughout the first half, trailing Iowa 7–0 late in the second quarter. The Irish finally got going, but found themselves on the Hawkeyes 12-yard line in the waning seconds of the half without any timeouts remaining.

The Notre Dame players knew exactly how to respond.

Irish left tackle Frank Varrichione let out a blood-curdling scream and collapsed to the turf, seemingly suffering a very sudden and mortal injury. Under existing college football rules, the officials were obligated to stop the clock and allow Varrichione to be helped off the field.

The Irish offense took advantage of the stoppage in play to line up, and on the final play of the half, Ralph Guglielmi threw a 12-yard touchdown pass to Dan Shannon, tying the score.

Notre Dame trailed Iowa 14–7 in the closing seconds of the fourth quarter. Again, the Irish were driving toward the Hawkeyes end zone. Again, Notre Dame was out of timeouts.

According to Leahy's script, this time it was the job of the right tackle to "suffer" an injury. So with six seconds remaining in the game and the ball on Iowa 9, Art Hunter took his turn.

The officials stopped the clock and, again, Guglielmi threw to Shannon in the end zone. Don Schaefer's extra point allowed Notre Dame to escape with a 14–14 tie.

"I thought Forest Evashevski was going to come across the field and kill Leahy," laughs John Lattner, Notre Dame's Heisman Trophy–winning halfback that season.

Perhaps it was the missed opportunity to defeat the number one team in the nation, but in his anger, Evashevski seemed to forget that many teams, including Iowa, used a similar play. Or perhaps it was the fact that Notre Dame was good enough to score touchdowns immediately following both feigned injuries. As Guglielmi puts it, "We still had to perform."

In explaining the Irish "strategy," Varrichione admits that Notre Dame's execution against Iowa was good, but not quite perfect.

"Normally, I'd be blocking somebody, and there would be a big pileup at the end of the play, so I'd just lay there and pretend to be injured," reveals Varrichione.

"But on the previous play, I had made my block and I saw the ball bouncing out of bounds. I thought the official had stopped the clock. We were walking back after the play, and Ralph said to me, 'Why didn't you fake an injury?'

"We were trying to call a play, and I saw the clock ticking down so I knew I had to stop the clock. So I just dropped at the line of scrimmage just like I dead out fainted."

Evashevski wasn't the only person outraged by the Irish ploy, as it turns out. Although the tactic was legal and widely used, many sportswriters criticized Notre Dame.

As Varrichione puts it, "Notre Dame being Notre Dame, we got a lot of criticism. I got letters from hundreds of fans. If they were Catholic, they thought I should be the next pope. Other people called me every name in the book."

The controversy brought about two changes. Most immediately, Notre Dame was dropped to second behind Maryland in both the Associated Press and United Press polls, and the NCAA eventually modified the rules to prohibit teams from using injuries to stop the clock at the end of each half.

Unfortunately, another 1953 practice no longer in existence today probably cost the '53 Irish a unanimous national championship. Notre Dame rebounded from the tie against Iowa to finish the season with a 9-0-1 record. Although Notre Dame's policy prohibited playing in bowl games during that era, Maryland did play in the Orange Bowl. Oklahoma, which Notre Dame had defeated in the season opener, beat the Terrapins 7-0.

But the Associated Press and the United Press still were conducting their final polls before the bowl games were played, so Maryland finished number one in each of those polls, despite finishing its season with a loss. Notre Dame, however, was declared as the national champion by at least 10 recognized selectors.

Among those crowning the '53 Irish champions was the presti-gious Helms Foundation, which picked its national champion after the bowl games were played.

No less an authority than Frank Leahy himself recognized the greatness of that team, calling the '53 squad his best-ever college-age team (Leahy's most powerful Notre Dame teams of the late '40s contained a mix of returning World War II veterans and younger players).

The huge shadow cast by the story of the "Fainting Irish," as some critics dubbed Notre Dame following the Iowa game, tends to obscure a remarkable season. Not only did the Irish post an undefeated record against top-flight competition, but they also had to deal with Leahy's rapidly deteriorating health.

The situation became a full-blown crisis against Georgia Tech. The Ramblin' Wreck arrived at Notre Dame Stadium riding a 31-game unbeaten streak and with a number four ranking in the polls. The Irish had eked out a 7–0 halftime lead when Leahy's health took a sudden and dramatic turn for the worse.

But despite what at least one Irish player initially thought, Leahy's condition wasn't taken out of the same chapter of the Notre Dame playbook as stopping the clock by faking an injury.

Lattner was a Chicago native and a long-time Notre Dame fol-lower. He was well aware that Leahy had learned well from his mentor Knute Rockne the art of going to great lengths to motivate his players. When Lattner first heard that Leahy had taken ill, he didn't believe it.

"I thought, 'He's pulling a Rockne,'" remembers Lattner. "I was laughing when somebody told us Leahy had a heart attack."

Doctors later determined that Leahy had not suffered a heart attack, but instead acute pancreatitis. Nonetheless, Leahy's con-dition was so grave that last rites were administered in the Notre Dame locker room. His players, properly concerned, defeated Georgia Tech 27–14.

Leahy was hospitalized but monitored Notre Dame's practices from his hospital bed via closed-circuit television. None of his players were surprised.

"Leahy and his staff were great at preparing us for games," says Guglielmi. "Our coolness under fire became natural because we had tougher situations during our scrimmages than anything we faced during the games.

To a man, Leahy's players describe him as a teacher without equal.

Leahy's doctors did not permit him to accompany the Irish to Los Angeles, where Notre Dame dismantled 20th-ranked Southern California 48–14. Leahy was back on the Notre Dame sideline two weeks after the attack, directing the Irish to a 40–14 victory over SMU.

Although not even Leahy knew it at the time, it would be the last game he ever coached. His doctors told Leahy he risked his life if he did not take it easy. Leahy knew that his own nature wouldn't permit easing up as Notre Dame's head coach, so he resigned.

"He was 47 years old when he left Notre Dame, but he looked like he was 67," said Lattner.

It may strike some as unfair that such an accomplished team—Lattner and Guglielmi are both members of the National Football Foundation College Football Hall of Fame—is perhaps best remembered for the Iowa game, but the players seem to understand it.

"It was our legacy," says guard Jack Lee.

Most of the players remember the game with laughter. Varrichione notes that Hunter's faked injury at the end of the second half didn't draw nearly the attention that Varrichione's performance did.

"I guess he did a better job of faking than I did," Varrichione chuckles. "Sportswriters came up to me and asked if I was really hurt. I said to them, 'If you looked up and saw Notre Dame losing 7–0, wouldn't you feel bad?'"

More than 50 years later, Guglielmi listed the Iowa game as his single-greatest memory from that season.

"Unfortunately, the game that stands out the most wasn't a win, but it was a tie," he says. "But coming back as we did in that game speaks to what an outstanding team we were."

It was an outstanding team, a final edition worthy of Leahy's legacy at Notre Dame. In addition to winning the Heisman Trophy, Lattner was a two-time winner of the Maxwell Award, presented by the Memorial Football Club of Philadelphia to the nation's best player. Lattner, Hunter, and end Don Penza were named All-Americans in '53. Over 20 members of the '53 squad played professional football—three players were drafted in the first round of the NFL draft following the '53 season, and three more were drafted in the first round the following year.

Longtime Notre Dame associate athletics director and sports information director Roger Valdiserri was a classmate of Lattner's. He considers the '53 backfield of Guglielmi, Lattner, Neil Worden, and Joe Heap (a three-time, first-team Academic All-American) as good as any that Notre Dame has ever fielded.

"Neil Worden was the best back in Notre Dame history not to make All-American," says Valdiserri.

Lattner echoed that theme.

"Any of those other three guys could have won the Heisman," he says. "I don't know how I got involved."

Guglielmi, who finished fourth in the voting for the '54 Heisman Trophy as a senior, returned the compliment.

"It was a privilege to play with Johnny Lattner," said Guglielmi. "He made me a better player."

Those on the team considered it a privilege to play at Notre Dame and for Frank Leahy.

"Notre Dame was the place to play college football in those days," Guglielmi says. "It was really something special. Today, you've got other programs that can say the same thing."

When the '53 Irish look back, they remind each other just how special they were.

"The stories get bigger every time we get together," says Lattner.

They may indeed get bigger, as the passage of time dulls the sharp edges of the controversies that surrounded the '53 team, but the record book speaks clearly to the accomplishments of those players.

There is little doubt that the '53 Irish were the best team in the country that season. There is absolutely no doubt they were a worthy end to Leahy's incredible run as Notre Dame's head coach, and a wonderful reflection on the University of Notre Dame.

chapter 4
The Terry Brennan Years

Terry Brennan, a star on three of Frank Leahy's post-WWII teams, took the head coaching reins from Leahy in 1954. Photo courtesy of AP/Wide World Photos.

Terry Brennan's 1957 Notre Dame team ended the longest streak in the history of college football—47 straight victories by Oklahoma—when his Irish traveled to Norman and shut out the Sooners 7–0.

Catching Up with...Terry Brennan

It's unlikely that recent games between Notre Dame and Army are etched in college football lore like the scoreless tie between the two teams in 1946. Similarly, it's a good bet that most games won't match the significance of the 1947 game.

But that doesn't mean Terry Brennan isn't watching intently.

A three-year starter at halfback on Frank Leahy's celebrated post–World War II Notre Dame teams, Brennan helped save the day in the '46 game between number one Army and number two Notre Dame at Yankee Stadium. After Johnny Lujack's famous touchdown-saving, open-field tackle of Heisman Trophy winner Doc Blanchard, the Cadets continued to march to the Notre Dame 11. But Brennan intercepted a halfback option pass thrown by Army's other eventual Heisman Trophy winner, Glenn Davis.

The following season, Brennan returned the game's opening kickoff for a touchdown, sparking a 27–7 rout in Notre Dame Stadium. The Irish went on to finish the season 9–0, claiming their second straight national title.

"Those were big, big games," recalls Brennan. "I still see Johnny Lujack and a lot of the rest of the guys, and those games seem like just yesterday."

Over the years, Brennan renewed acquaintances with legendary Army head coach Red Blaik and many of the former Cadet players.

"When we played, they were like mortal enemies," chuckles Brennan. "But once you get to know them, they're pretty good guys."

Brennan recalls sharing lunch with Blaik and famed sportswriter Red Smith. They reminisced about missed opportunities for both teams in the epic scoreless tie in '46. Blaik wrapped up the postmortem succinctly: "He said, 'You're right, we both screwed up.' "

After winning three straight city championships at Mount Carmel High School in Chicago, Brennan returned to Notre Dame in 1953 to coach the freshman squad under Leahy. He succeeded Leahy as head coach in 1954, and his five-year 32–18 record included 9–1 and 8–2 records his first two seasons that ranked the Irish fourth and ninth, respectively, in the final Associated Press polls.

Following his coaching tenure, Brennan worked as an expert commentator during football telecasts. He continues to watch games with an analytical perspective.

"It's inevitable, having played and coached for so many years," Brennan says.

Brennan offers a different view from those who claim college football is radically different than it was in the '40s and '50s.

"It really hasn't changed much at all, other than the fact that we had that silly one-platoon game when I was coaching," he says.

"But they just use different names for the same defenses," Brennan explains.

"We used to play a 6–1 defense, but our ends played both ways, and were able to drop off into pass coverage, so it was just like a 4–3 today."

After retiring from the financial industry, Brennan bought a network of sports talk radio stations with one of his sons. Since selling the network, Brennan spends most of his time attending sporting events and music recitals—juggling his schedule to keep up with six children, 24 grandchildren, and two great-grandchildren, all living in the general vicinity of his suburban Chicago home.

"It's great when you're no longer paying the tuition," he laughs.

Golden Anniversary for the Golden Boy

Often imitated in title but never duplicated on or off the field, Paul Hornung remains Notre Dame's original "Golden Boy."

That same title was bestowed upon Rick Mirer by *Sports Illustrated* in 1990 when the sophomore's initial start resulted in a 28–24 victory over Michigan. Like Hornung, Mirer possesses blond coifs. Like Hornung, Mirer was recruited as a quarterback.

However, there can be only one original. Hornung is also an original in that there never was and never will be a Heisman Trophy winner like him.

Today, there are three unofficial stipulations needed to receive the award.

1. Playing for a national title contender or at least a team ranked in the top 10. Thirteen of the last 16 recipients played on teams with zero or just one loss at the time of the voting, and none had a worse record than 8–3.
2. Impressive, if not gaudy, statistics, preferably on offense.
3. Defining games on television that capture the nation's imagination.

On December 5, 1956, those three criteria were rendered meaningless when Hornung captured the most coveted individual prize in college athletics. His 1,066 points in the balloting edged Tennessee's Johnny Majors's 994 for top honors.

Playing for a national title contender?

In 1956 Notre Dame had its worst season ever, finishing 2–8 while getting outscored 289–130. Meanwhile, Majors had led Tennessee to a 10–1 regular-season mark and a number two finish nationally, behind Oklahoma.

Finishing third and fourth in the Heisman balloting were two Oklahoma products, Tom McDonald and Jerry Tubbs, who led the Sooners to their third consecutive unbeaten season and second straight national title.

No way that could happen today.

How about posting mind-boggling stats?

Hornung's numbers in 1956 were relatively modest. As a quarterback, he completed 59 of 111 passes (53.1 percent) for 917 yards, 13 interceptions, and only three touchdowns.

Compare that to Stanford's John Brodie, who finished seventh in the '56 balloting: 139 of 240 (57.9 percent) for 1,633 yards, 14 interceptions, and 12 touchdowns. (Stanford finished 4–6.)

Hornung also rushed for 420 yards on 94 attempts (4.5 yards per carry)—plus he intercepted two passes and kicked 14 extra points.

Still, Syracuse's Jim Brown and Oklahoma's McDonald had more glittering numbers. Brown gained 986 yards on 158 carries (6.2 yards per carry), scored 14 touchdowns, kicked 22 extra points, and recorded three interceptions. McDonald rushed for 853 yards on 119 attempts (7.2 yards per carry) and scored 12 touchdowns.

No way that could happen today.

As for "defining" games for a national audience—such as Tim Brown's two punt returns for scores against Michigan State in 1987—Hornung had nothing of the sort.

The Irish had one game nationally televised in 1956—the 40–0 whitewashing by Oklahoma in Notre Dame Stadium. The two games that were regionally televised resulted in a 33–7 pummeling at the hands of Navy and a 47–14 thrashing from Michigan State.

A 2–8 record, good but not sparkling stats, no defining moments on national television—and yet Hornung won the Heisman.

In addition to Majors, McDonald, Tubbs, Brown, and Brodie, future All-Pros Ron Kramer (Michigan) and Jim Parker (Ohio State) finished in the top eight.

"I can't believe it," Hornung said at the time. "I didn't think I was even up for consideration."

Of course, it was a different era. There was no weekly "Heisman Watch," and candidates weren't flown into New York City for the dramatic nationally televised announcement. Hornung said he first heard about it in a phone call from former winner and then radio broadcaster Tom Harmon.

"I was told to go to [Notre Dame sports publicity director] Charlie Callahan's office," Hornung recalled. "When I got there, Charlie handed me the phone and said, 'Tell your mother you have just won the Heisman Trophy.'"

How did Hornung win the '56 Heisman?

Undoubtedly, the name Notre Dame had much to do with it. Hornung became the fifth Fighting Irish recipient in 13 seasons, beginning with Angelo Bertelli (1943) and continuing with John Lujack (1947), Leon Hart (1949), and John Lattner (1953).

Second, Hornung had a stellar junior year, leading the Irish to an 8–2 mark and finishing fifth in the Heisman race. Voters kept that in mind for 1956.

Finally, football grants-in-aid had been cut back at Notre Dame in the early 1950s, and the roster had become thinner under third-year head coach Terry Brennan, who had succeeded the legendary Frank Leahy. With Notre Dame bereft of the depth it once had, Hornung became the most versatile player in college football.

In 1956 Hornung led the Irish in seven statistical categories, and only Brodie ranked ahead of him nationally in total yards. In addition, Hornung was second nationally in kickoff returns, 15th in passing, and 16th in scoring.

He lined up at quarterback, fullback, and halfback, played through several injuries, kicked off and kicked extra points, punted, accounted for more than half of the team's scoring (including all

Paul Hornung strikes a Heisman pose after receiving the trophy at the Downtown Athletic Club in New York City on December 12, 1956.
Photo courtesy of AP/Wide World Photos.

the points in the 21–14 victory over North Carolina), and was second in tackles recorded (55).

The esteemed and late Dick Schaap wrote: "In recent years many schools have had football teams named Desire. In 1956 Notre Dame had a football team named Hornung. He passed. He tackled. He intercepted passes. Surrounded by the walking wounded, playing for a team crippled by injuries, Hornung was the whole show."

Amid the worst of circumstances, something special was sensed even then about Hornung, a bonus pick by the hapless Green Bay Packers in the 1957 NFL draft.

With Vince Lombardi's hiring in 1959, Hornung moved from quarterback to halfback and became the centerpiece of one of the great dynasties in sports history. Hornung led the league in scoring from 1959 to 1961, and he was on four Packers teams that won NFL titles.

"The thing I'm proudest of is that I made the College Hall of Fame as a quarterback and the Pro Hall of Fame as a running back," Hornung said.

His exploits off the field made the "Golden Boy" a legend in other ways. Well before "Broadway Joe's" arrival at New York, Hornung's nocturnal lifestyle was there for public consumption.

"Never get married in the morning—you never know who you'll meet that night," Hornung once said, but he is now married for a couple of decades to wife, Angela.

After repeatedly fining Hornung for his late-night shenanigans, the exasperated taskmaster Lombardi finally decided to raise the fine to a much higher level.

"And if you find anyone worth that much, call me," Lombardi reportedly told Hornung.

Hornung has said that he would like his epitaph to read: "He went though life on scholarship."

In 1956 and beyond, though, he earned everything he received, including the Heisman.

chapter 5
The Ara Parseghian Years

Ara Parseghian celebrates his first victory as Notre Dame's head coach as he is carried on the shoulders of his players after the Irish defeated Wisconsin 31–7 at Madison on September 26, 1964.

Ara Parseghian served as architect for one of the most amazing turnarounds in college football history in 1964 when he took over an Irish program that had finished 2–7 in 1963 and led them to a 9–1 season and to within minutes of winning the national championship.

Magical 1964 Season Marked Debut of Era of Ara

Notre Dame's storied football history includes 11 consensus national championships and five other seasons when the Irish finished number two in the national polls. Yet another season that falls outside those 16—the 9–1 campaign of 1964—always will be considered one of the finest seasons in Notre Dame football history.

The reason that such lofty status is heaped upon the 1964 season involves not so much the final record as it does the circumstances leading up to that memorable fall. The Irish program had experienced an unthinkable slump, without a winning season in the five-year stretch from 1959 to 1963, and a new coaching staff led by Ara Parseghian had been called in to right the ship on the heels of a dismal 2–7 showing in 1963.

The bar of expectations for 1964 was set low for traditional Notre Dame standards, as many of the Irish faithful would be content with the "baby steps" progress of simply compiling a winning record. "Six-and-four in '64" became a common catchphrase among alums...but there certainly was the fear of yet another season in which the Irish failed to win more games than they lost.

The Irish—playing for their third head coach in as many seasons—opened the year with the additional hurdle of playing on the road, but Parseghian's mastery had his team clicking from the get-go in a 31–7 rout of Wisconsin. The win vaulted Notre Dame to ninth in the AP poll, and the Irish then climbed to the sixth, fourth, and second spots after wins over Purdue (34–15), at Air Force (34–7), and back at home against UCLA (24–0).

Two more wins over Stanford (28–6) and the Roger Staubach–led Navy squad (40–0, in Philadelphia) preceded a 17–15 escape at Pittsburgh that pushed Notre Dame up to the number one ranking for the first time in a decade. A couple more wins over Michigan State (28–0) and Iowa (28–0) followed, but a heartbreaking loss at USC (20–17) prevented the Irish from claiming what would have been a storybook national championship (Notre Dame did not compete in postseason bowls at that time).

When the dust had settled, Notre Dame stunningly had set 27 team records and tied two others—as the Irish coupled a record-setting aerial attack (2,015 total passing yards) with the nation's second-ranked rush defense (68.7 yards per game) while finishing third in the final national polls.

Nine individuals who were participants or close observers in that season have provided their insights into what Parseghian did to "make that season click." They dissect his leadership style and highlight some of the key decisions that made the debut season in the "Era of Ara" one that never should be forgotten.

The comments included below come from nine individuals, one for each win of the '64 season: two leading players on that 1964 team (Heisman Trophy–winning quarterback John Huarte and captain Jim Carroll), assistant coaches Tom Pagna and Johnny Ray, graduate assistant coach Brian Boulac, team radio analyst Jim Morse, longtime *South Bend Tribune* writer Joe Doyle, legendary Notre Dame fencing coach Mike DeCicco (who also worked closely with the football team in '64 as its academic advisor), and a spirited student from the early 1960s, Russell "Cappy" Gagnon, now a security specialist at his alma mater. All of the above individuals, with the exception of Pagna, have the added perspective of being Notre Dame graduates and, with the exception of DeCicco and Gagnon, most also played football for the Irish.

Parseghian had been a successful coach at his alma mater Miami of Ohio (1951–1955) and Northwestern (1956–1963), and he brought two assistants with him to Notre Dame—Richard "Doc" Urich (ends and offensive line coach) and Paul Shoults (defensive backs)—who had been on his staffs at both of the previous schools. Pagna, who had played for Parseghian at Miami, also came along from the staff at Northwestern and coached the offensive backfield.

The other five coaches on the 1964 staff all were former Notre Dame players. Ray, brought in to coach the defensive linemen and linebackers, was a South Bend native and had served five years as head coach of one of the nation's top defensive teams at John Carroll University. Joe Yonto had been head coach at Notre Dame

High School in Niles, Illinois, and would assist with the defensive line. The other three—Dave Hurd (assisted with offensive line), George Sefcik (head freshman coach), and John Murphy (assistant freshman coach)—all had been retained from the 1963 staff, providing Parseghian with a link for perspective on the previous seasons.

"Ara did a great job of balancing that staff, and we worked well together as a team of coaches. It was a very strong staff from the top down," says Pagna.

"He told his assistants, 'Loyalty is a two-way street,' and there was great mutual respect among all of us. He was a dynamic personality and commanded your attention. If you had an idea, he heard it out—and might make it better. As a member of that staff, you wanted to be a contributor."

A common theme when discussing the dawning of the Era of Ara is the coach's unquestioned ability to inspire his players with newfound confidence.

"Ara had a knack for developing a lot of pride in yourself and in the team. He simply came in and rebuilt our confidence from day one," says Carroll. "Ara was such a devoted coach and he had that great love of the game that was contagious. He sold us on the fact we should be confident in ourselves."

According to Doyle, the first-year Irish coach "had confidence in his own ability and it easily permeated the entire squad."

It also swept across a campus starving for a return to glory on the gridiron. "When Ara arrived, it was like a big breath of fresh air," says Gagnon. "He took us out of the wilderness."

"The success of that 1964 season happened in stages. And as a new coach, Ara had to establish discipline with that team," says Boulac, who had wrapped up his career as a member of the floundering 1963 squad.

The mantra of discipline extended to all phases of the football players' lives—practice, games, academics, and social life.

"When Ara was at Northwestern, he felt that Notre Dame had better players but would lose on a fumble or bad penalty," remembers Gagnon. "It was basically a lack of discipline, and he set out to change that from the start."

Morse often spoke with fellow Muskegon, Michigan, native Bill Wolski (a fullback on the '64 team) and asked about the change in practice sessions under the new coach. "He said it was like night and day. Everything they did in practice had a purpose and there was no wasted time," says Morse.

The 1964 spring season featured a clear message from the head coach: no players on the team were to run into trouble at any of the local South Bend taverns.

"It happened to a guy on the team, probably our best pro prospect, and he was kicked off the team," says Boulac. "Kids saw that the man meant what he said. He stood by his guns."

The high level of discipline also extended to the academic realm. After meeting with executive vice president Father Edmund Joyce, C.S.C., and DeCicco, Ara had a familiar message for his team.

"He told those kids that they had to follow the academic guidelines as they were outlined or they wouldn't play," says DeCicco. "And the first kid who stepped on the cracks, Ara booted him off the field. There was complete discipline.

"That message spread through the team like it was cancer. Those kids straightened out and flew right. Ara told us he respected what Notre Dame meant on the academic side even more than athletically. Everyone thinks that coaches always are looking for ways to beat the system, but that was not Ara's way of doing things."

All of the confidence and discipline in the world may not have added up to a nine-win season. But Parseghian added another wrinkle to his coaching genius by pulling the right strings with several key position switches—in addition to the pivotal moment in which he selected a starting quarterback.

Huarte logged just 50 combined minutes of playing time in the '62 and '63 seasons and had yet to earn a varsity monogram. He had an unconventional style, but there were things Parseghian liked about him—namely his dodging feet and a quick release—and Parseghian declared Huarte the starter at the end of spring ball. He envisioned the California product leading his team to great heights the following fall.

One of the key position shifts produced Huarte's favorite target, as Jack Snow dropped 15 pounds and converted from fullback to receiver. Snow went on to set three Irish single-season records and finished fifth in the Heisman voting, even garnering Doyle's first-place vote for the nation's top award.

The holdover "Elephant Backfield"—comprised of halfbacks Paul Costa (240 pounds), Jim Snowden (250), and fullback Pete Duranko (235)—also was disbanded, with each moving to the line (Snowden on the offensive side and the others on the defensive). Duranko and Snowden enjoyed pro careers thanks to the switch, with Duranko also earning All-America honors as a member of the fearsome defensive-line foursome that helped the Irish win the 1966 national title.

Rule changes had introduced two-platoon football for the 1964 season, and Parseghian also shined in this regard by placing players on their most effective side of the ball. Huarte and Snow were anchored on the offensive team, while players such as defensive lineman Alan Page and linebacker Jim Lynch were free to focus on the start of their tremendous All-America careers as elite defensive players.

"I've known every Notre Dame head coach since Frank Leahy, and none has been as thoroughly prepared and organized as Ara," says Morse. "He could adjust to the situation and put people in the right positions. He led virtually the same players from a 2–7 season to a 9–1 record the next year."

Adds Huarte, "From a psychological standpoint, Ara was very smart in how he handled the players. In my case, he told me to just go out there and play and if I made mistakes they were going to stick with me. He also was very good at using players in the scope of their skill levels. He just was outstanding in developing his offensive scheme to maximize the personnel."

Parseghian and his staff used several tactics—such as computerized scouting, quartering the team at nearby Moreau Seminary the night before home games, and heading to Phoenix a day early before moving on to USC—that were new to Notre Dame and, in some cases, on the cutting edge nationwide. He also was not afraid to insert himself into drills on a regular basis, strengthening the bonds between player and coach. "They had never heard of the two-minute drill at Notre Dame before Ara got there," says Doyle. "He would simulate the drill and control the clock. One time they scored six straight times, and on the seventh drive Ara jumped out there and kicked the field goal. He just really got into the spirit of the thing."

The first-year Irish coach also would run goal-line scrimmages at every practice and in general had full knowledge of everything that was going on at each position. "Ara knew both sides of the ball like a book, and it was like he was the coordinator on both sides," says Doyle.

Adds Ray, "Ara truly was a hands-on coach who knew his Xs and Os and knew the psychology of how to handle a team. He even would lead the warm-up exercises—the players would respect him even more for things like that."

Gagnon was just as impressed the day after games as he was on Saturdays. "Starting with that 1964 season, Ara would do a Sunday afternoon TV show and he would break down the plays from the day before," says Gagnon. "Just watching that, it was clear that he knew his stuff."

Parseghian's intense approach to his job provided great inspiration to players and fans alike.

"Ara was such a great motivator who pushed the right buttons," says Boulac. "After the first game when everything we did was right, the kids believed in everything he said. It was such an emotional season and we exploded on the scene."

Adds Ray, "Ara had such a thorough and intelligent way of doing things. It showed the type of person he was. If he was in business, he would have been a top CEO or president of some great company."

Like many great leaders, Parseghian had a depth to his personality that often went unperceived by the general public.

"Most people never really saw what a great sense of humor Ara had," says Ray. "He was very intense on the sideline and in preparing the team but he also was great at using that intensity to set up his funny side."

A common phrase among the Irish coaches was "Ara is putting the 'gig' on you," in reference to one of the coach's classic practical jokes. On one such occasion, he instructed Boulac to load up some free weights at the bottom of one assistant's travel bag. He then called that coach into the locker room and gave him a spirited pep talk for the ensuing recruiting trip.

"Ara's voice was getting that crescendo and he keeps saying things like 'You can't fail' and 'Do you understand?'" recalls Ray. "And then he tells the coach to pick up his bag and get going, and the guy was so excited he ran five steps before falling down like a sack of potatoes because of the weights.

"But that was the thing about Ara. He was very clever and intelligent with his humor and it helped keep all of us loose at the right times."

In his book, aptly titled *Era of Ara*, Pagna wrote that athletics was the lifeblood of Notre Dame and "Ara provided the transfusion." It truly was a magical season in 1964, setting the stage for national championship seasons in '66 and '73.

Ara, Can You Really Stop That Snow?

If you're ever wondering about the power of the Notre Dame head coaching position, consider the story former Irish offensive coordinator Tom Pagna often tells about Ara Parseghian. Nine straight victories to start Parseghian's first season in 1964 proved to be a powerful elixir for the Irish students—so much so that at a late-season home game after snow began to fall, the students began chanting, "Ara, stop the snow! Ara, stop the snow!" Ara's feigned response? "That's ridiculous. Do you think I *could*?" Some years later, and with Parseghian now boasting a national title on his résumé, the same chant rang out at another November home contest. This time, Ara's query was, "Do you think I *should*?"

John Huarte: Timing Matters

"Lack of a consistently good quarterback could again prevent Notre Dame from having a successful season." —1963 *Notre Dame Football Review*, previewing the 1964 season

It took 41 years before John Huarte was inducted into the College Football Hall of Fame in 2005.

While it's unusual for a Heisman Trophy recipient to have to wait so long, if anybody can appreciate the virtue of patience—and timing—it's Huarte.

Entering his senior year at Notre Dame in 1964, Huarte had not even played enough college football to earn a school monogram, never mind be a bona fide candidate for the sport's most prestigious individual award. Never before—and never since—has one college football player emerged so dramatically from obscurity one season to prominence the next. Oklahoma State's Barry Sanders also was a bit of a late bloomer in 1988, but even he had accumulated nearly 1,000 yards rushing in his earlier years while backing up Thurman Thomas.

Quarterback John Huarte was prepared when his opportunity finally came along, and he utilized the same disciplined preparedness to become one of the most successful businessmen of his time.

But Huarte had logged approximately five minutes' playing time as a sophomore for a 5–5 team in 1962, and during the 2–7 implosion in 1963, Huarte finished the season as the number three quarterback, behind Frank Budka and Sandy Bonvechio, and barely ahead of Denis Szot, who had started that year's opener.

Yet with the arrival of first-year head coach Ara Parseghian in 1964, Huarte led a renaissance that resulted in a number three national finish in 1964 and laid the groundwork for future prosperity.

Luck and timing are vital components in life, but for more than four decades Huarte has preached a corollary to his message. "Sometimes when I talk to young people, I tell them my story and they're quite amazed," Huarte said. "But a lot of it is you have to be prepared when an opportunity comes along, too."

Huarte has experienced a Heisman-like career in his personal and professional exploits as well. Currently the owner/CEO of Arizona Tile Company, he has seen his business, the largest importer of granite in North America, branch out from Phoenix to Denver, Oakland, and San Diego, with offices in several different continents.

The father of five grown children, Huarte has been married for more than 40 years to wife Eileen. He views his role as a grandparent of nine as his greatest celebration.

His Cinderella 1964 campaign isn't far behind.

The Anaheim, California, product enrolled in 1961 from Mater Dei High, but it wasn't until the spring of 1964 that new Irish mentor Ara Parseghian found the diamond amidst the Irish scrap heap, as well as many others such as little-used halfback Jack Snow (three carries, 26 yards), who was shifted to split end.

In the 1964 opener alone Huarte passed for 270 yards, highlighted by 61- and 42-yard scoring tosses to Snow, who would finish fifth in the Heisman balloting. The two continued to thrive, and a new Irish legend was born en route to a 9–0 start and number one ranking.

"There can be a tendency in sports to think all good things come from yourself," Huarte said. "When you really look at it, it takes a lot of forces on the outside—coaches, opportunity, teammates—to make it happen.

"I did a lot of basic work to develop the fundamental skills, and then was very fortunate to have Ara come along. Fortune in sports is strange. A lot of it is being at the right place at the right time."

As a second-round draft choice of the AFL's New York Jets in 1965, Huarte signed a $200,000 deal on January 9. One week earlier, the Jets signed a rookie named Joe Namath, injured most of his senior year at Alabama, for $427,000.

John Huarte averaged 10.05 yards per pass attempt during his senior year—a Notre Dame record that still stands (minimum 100 attempts). His 205 attempts resulted in 2,062 yards. Kevin McDougal's 1993 season is a distant second (9.69 yards per attempt).

"That was really a business deal," explained Huarte of his contract. "Notre Dame was the best draw in New York at that time. I was drafted high by the Jets and helped them sell about 40,000 season tickets that year. It was a commercial transaction."

Huarte never played a minute in his one season at New York, but his own greatest transaction was made there when he met Eileen Marie Devine during an elevator ride in the Big Apple. The stunning Devine actually had been asked out by Namath on a couple of occasions, but she politely declined.

How many people in history can say they not only won the Heisman but also married a woman Namath attempted to woo?

Huarte was then traded to the Boston Patriots, where he backed up Babe Parilli. He remained a journeyman behind people such as Len Dawson for the 1970 Kansas City Super Bowl champs before retiring from the soon-to-be-defunct World Football League in 1975.

In the NFL, Huarte completed 19 of 48 (39.6 percent) pass attempts for 230 yards and one touchdown, thereby earning the rap as a Heisman bust. But if marrying the woman of your dreams, attaining financial wealth, and winning a Super Bowl ring during your pro career is a disappointment, millions of males would jump at the chance to sign up for such failure.

"Most pros play maybe two or three years," Huarte reflected. "I was fortunate to get 10 years out of it and make more money as a young married man than doing anything else. Then I closed the door and put all my energies into business."

Proud of his Notre Dame education and the school's values, Huarte cherishes his moments back on campus and at the Hall of Fame. Both places are about achieving dreams, and Huarte has fulfilled his.

The Heisman Trophy winner in 1964, John Huarte was the sixth Notre Dame player to win the award over a 22-year span, starting in 1943.

"The Hall of Fame Foundation does an unknown amount of good for young people, giving them the idea—that little sparkle in the eyes—that maybe I can do that," Huarte said. "Planting that seed of hope is absolutely crucial."

Being prepared for that moment when hope arrives, as Huarte was in 1964, is just as important.

10 Questions with John Huarte

There are three amazing Horatio Alger–type stories in Notre Dame's history at quarterback.

In 1993 Kevin McDougal, a nondescript player for three years behind Rick Mirer and expected to play behind freshman Ron Powlus, took the throttle and became the school's career-pass efficiency king while leading Notre Dame to an 11–1 record and number two finish.

In 1977 third-team quarterback Joe Montana, who sat out the 1976 season with a shoulder injury, was inserted in the third game when the Irish trailed by 10 points in the fourth quarter at Purdue. He rallied the Irish to victory and steered them to the national title.

And in 1964 John Huarte, who finished the previous year as the third-team quarterback, emerged to win the Heisman Trophy and guide the Irish to a 9–0 start a year after Notre Dame was 2–7.

Huarte recalls his introduction to Notre Dame, the dramatic Cinderella campaign, and his relationship with the late Jack Snow, who shattered the school records that year for single-season receptions (60), yards (1,114), and touchdown receptions (nine) en route to finishing fifth in the Heisman.

Question: How did you get introduced to Notre Dame, and what would prompt you to matriculate there from California when the Irish were in their dark age of football?

John Huarte: My introduction came by radio when I was about 12 years old or so, sitting on an irrigation ditch on a farm on a Saturday, listening to some far-off team called Notre Dame. Then I'd ask my dad and he'd explain who it was.

There was some history. My high school coach had gone to Notre Dame. My brother, David (class of 1960), was in geology at Notre Dame. The head coach, Joe Kuharich, had also recruited heavily in California: Tommy MacDonald, Daryle Lamonica, Jack Snow, Nick Eddy, myself, a few others. So the distance wasn't really unusual in my mind. I had dreamed of going to Notre Dame and maybe playing football there. The fact that Notre Dame was struggling—well, maybe they needed some better players and I might be able to help. I didn't really think too much about that.

Q: During your senior year in high school, Notre Dame was 2–8, the same record it had four years earlier. During your fresh-man year in 1961, Notre Dame lost five of its last seven games. In 1962 the team finished 5–5 and in 1963 it was 2–7. What was the atmosphere like?

JH: After I arrived at Notre Dame, I remember it was quite common that there were articles in the newspapers and around campus that maybe Notre Dame should de-emphasize football because they couldn't play with the big schools. I was kind of sur-prised about that. Being a young person, it's pretty hard to measure that.

I was just thinking of an opportunity for me to play. During my four years, it was hard for me to measure how good teams were and how good we were or weren't in comparison because this was the only place I had been. Gradually, over my freshman and sophomore years, I began thinking we had some pretty good talent. I kept thinking that it was a lot of small breakdowns that were causing us to lose games.

Q: During the 2–7 campaign in your junior year, you didn't play much and Jack Snow used to mention that you two would be on the sideline watching other teams hit on long passes and have nice passing attacks, and you'd say to each other, "We could do that."

JH: That's exactly true. In fact, I can remember one game in particular in 1962 when we played at Northwestern [a 35–6 Irish loss to the then–third-ranked Wildcats] when Ara Parseghian was coaching there. We were watching his quarterback, Tommy Myers, throw to a guy named Paul Flatley. Jack and I were not being used and, as we watched the other team advance the ball with the passing attack, we would kind of nod to each other with the full knowledge that we could do the same thing.

We sort of gave up on the forward pass there. When Ara came in, it was an entirely different program.

Q: When you saw the news that Ara was hired, was there a surge of excitement or did you feel that you'd be put on the shelf after not showing anything the first three years?

JH: I was just elated because what I had seen firsthand from his style of coaching, I knew it would be transferred to Notre Dame. I thought there was a strong possibility that we would get a chance to show our skills. That first spring, Ara knew very little about his players, so he was experimenting and moving a lot of people around. I was just one of many quarterbacks being considered. After a few weeks, he moved me to the first team. I was confident that we would move the ball and be successful.

A few days before our first game at Wisconsin, Ara made a commitment to me and basically said, "I'm going with you. You have the skills. If you make a mistake, don't worry about it. You're my quarterback." That was very smart for him to do at that time. I needed to hear that because I had not played much for three years.

Q: You had a shoulder injury in the closing days of that spring that was originally diagnosed as needing surgery. What happened?

JH: That was a dangerous situation—I had a separation in the collarbone of my throwing shoulder. My dad had been a pro baseball player who had a very good arm, and he knew you didn't want to be fiddling around with the joints of a throwing arm. You didn't have the advances in surgery back then as you do today.

The first three doctors said there had to be surgery. Ara Parseghian then asked [assistant coach] Tom Pagna to drive me to Chicago, where we could see a specialist friend of his from his days at Northwestern. The specialist's decision was the opposite of everyone else's. He said, "Just leave it alone and it will be fine." That was the course of action we took. If they had done surgery, you never would have heard of me. To aid the healing, I did a lot of swimming, rested, and in six to eight weeks it gradually returned to normal. I gradually did some easy throwing, and by the time fall came I was fine.

Q: *Jack Snow once said that before the team even met with Ara, the two of you marched into Ara's office and Jack laid it on the line, saying, "I'm the best damn receiver here and this is the best damn quarterback." Do you recall that meeting?*

JH (laughing): That's just the way it happened. Jack was kind of a saucy personality, and he coaxed me into going down there and talking to him. I think it was because we were ready to be seniors and for three years we had done hardly much of anything. He wanted to make a point for him to remember us. I can say that Jack was the ringleader of that conversation, and I just basically went along and seconded what he said. He did most of the talking for the two of us.

Q: *How did you and Jack develop such a close relationship? Was it just both having California ties?*

JH: We had gone to summer school and stayed out for hours passing and catching the ball, running patterns together. Jack took real pride in his work, and I was working on getting the ball there and the timing. Jack was doing most of the work with all the running. It was much easier for the quarterback to drop back about seven yards and deliver the ball. During summer school and even back in California, we'd have a lot of time working together. He was from Long Beach and I was from Anaheim, so that's only about 25 miles or less.

Q: Even though Ara won national titles in 1966 and 1973, he has said that 9–0 start in 1964 was the most joy he had as a coach because there were no expectations, and once success was tasted, everyone couldn't wait until the next day to get out there again. Would that be an accurate appraisal?

JH: It was very much like that. Ara also brought in an excellent team of assistants, a real good management group. Tom Pagna was the one who worked closely with me, along with Ara. The whole team was just hungry for leadership and Ara gave us that—plus we had pretty good talent that was excited about finally being able to display it.

Q: When and how did you find out about the Heisman?

A: It was a shout down the hall from a guy named George Keenen, who was a roommate of mine on the second floor in Walsh Hall. He answered the phone in our room and he shouted down the hall, "John, you got it!" I got on the phone and [sports information director] Charlie Callahan with his raspy voice confirmed that I had been awarded the Heisman Trophy and I would be going to New York with my parents. It was extremely exciting.

I think what happened is Notre Dame coming back from a poor record for a number of years just captured the imagination of the people throughout the country. We also had a national schedule, and we came back in a dramatic fashion.

Q: With the death of Jack Snow, did you feel you lost a piece of yourself?

JH: It was very difficult. I knew he had contacted the staph infection and I had been in touch through his daughter, Michelle, and his former roommate. We were all wondering whether he was going to recover, and at first the doctors thought he could. Then he had to go back in the hospital.... It was very difficult. You have those close memories and ties as young people playing college ball, the great turnaround. You go from not being recognized to playing in the pros—and he ended up having a heckuva pro career. We had a very special situation as a couple of California kids and how things turned out for us.

Remembering Dick Arrington

How good an athlete was the late Dick Arrington? Good enough to be selected Notre Dame's Athlete of the Year by the student body for the 1964–1965 season—in a sports year that also included Heisman Trophy winner John Huarte, All-American football end Jack Snow, and NCAA cross country individual runner-up Bill Clark. A three-year starter in football playing guard and tackle—at times on both offense and defense—Arrington also was a standout heavyweight wrestler for the Irish, finishing third in the 1965 NCAA finals.

Arrington's success at Notre Dame was due in no small part to his intelligence and his commitment to knowledge. "I really didn't have one particular college I wanted to come to after high school," Arrington said. "I had known some graduates before me who had gotten athletic scholarships to different colleges and did nothing but play sports. That didn't make much sense to me. If I spent four years just playing football, I would have nothing when those four years were over. If I spent those four years working in a factory for $4,000 a year, I could earn $16,000 to help my parents along.

"If I were going to go to college I had to get something out of it. So I came to Notre Dame. You hear a lot about athletes giving to their schools, but I can never forget that the most important thing is that I profit from Notre Dame.

"When people ask me how I can keep up with studies and play two sports [football and wrestling], I tell them I don't know. It's very hard for athletes around here to keep up with solid courses and also play.

"You have to have knowledge in the first place, but it will do you no good unless you learn to work yourself hard and not quit just because you are tired or sore.

"Everyone is basically lazy. We need someone or something to make us drive ourselves. Sports in college, like life, are not intended to be just fun. It's a lot harder to fight to win than to win."

Legendary Notre Dame coach Ara Parseghian acknowledged Arrington's contributions to the team and his dedication to the game, saying, "The moment Dick Arrington started working part-time with our defense in 1965, things started to shape up. Dick operated there as if he owned the position.

"After our game against California, we had been alternating Dick and Tom Regner as offensive guards with our second unit. On one occasion we sent Dick in quickly. He didn't have time to get his helmet strap fastened. He was still trying to get it fastened before the snap of the ball. He carried out his assignment with one hand, trying to fasten the snap with the other.

"As we noticed on film, Arrington ran the whole play, blocked out two men, but all the while didn't take his mind off one thing—fastening that helmet snap. Afterward he explained that 'Coach [Doc] Urich gets mad when we don't have our straps fastened.'"

Catching Up with...Larry Conjar

As his sophomore football season at Notre Dame wound down, things weren't going Larry Conjar's way.

"My dad was driving 560 miles each way to see me play, but I was selling programs outside the stadium on game day," says Conjar. "One Sunday afternoon, I sat by myself in the top row of the stadium and asked myself what in the world I was doing.

"And I don't know what possessed me, but I stood up and looked across the campus and said to myself that tomorrow night was going to be my night."

"Tomorrow night" was the weekly Monday night scrimmage between Conjar's scout team and the freshmen.

On the first play, Irish head coach Ara Parseghian called an off-tackle play. Conjar's assignment as fullback—block the defensive end. Conjar flattened him.

"Conjar, that's not bad," Parseghian said before calling the play three more times in succession. Each time, Conjar steamrolled the defensive end.

After the fourth time, Irish assistant coach Tom Pagna slapped Conjar on the rear and said, "Conjar, it's about time!"

Conjar won the starting fullback position in 1965 and earned third-team All-America honors in 1966. He was selected by Cleveland in the second round of the NFL draft.

Conjar showed similar persistence—with similar results—when a Saint Mary's College freshman running for homecoming queen caught his eye.

"I fell in love with a picture," he says. "But for a year, I was too afraid even to ask her friends to introduce me.

"Finally, she was on a date with Kenny Ivan, one of my teammates. I knew that if I went up to them, he'd have to introduce me. He did, and I never left her side."

Larry still carries that photo of Donna after more than 35 years of marriage. "It's been the best," he says.

After his NFL career was cut short due to a near-fatal bout with spinal meningitis, Conjar got into the real estate business. He and his wife now live in Evanston, Illinois, where Larry oversees a family-owned real estate business.

Conjar sees a great similarity between the character of Irish head coach Charlie Weis and Parseghian—and knows what a difference that can make in the lives of the players.

"The guy made me," says Conjar of Parseghian. "I wouldn't be who I am or where I am without him."

Catching Up with...Jim Lynch

The way Jim Lynch sees it, he had probably the only Irish-Catholic parents in the state of Ohio who might have had the slightest twinge of regret at his decision to accept a football scholarship from the University of Notre Dame.

Lynch's older brother, Tom, was a captain of Navy's 1963 football team, the last Navy squad to defeat Notre Dame. Navy coaches did their very best to persuade Jim to follow in Tom's footsteps.

But although the Midshipmen lost the contest to recruit Jim Lynch, they didn't lose one ounce of his respect. "Both [Notre Dame and Navy] stand for a whole lot more than just a place to go to school," says Lynch.

Lynch did follow in his brother's footsteps in one regard, as he went on to captain his team as a senior—Notre Dame's 1966 national championship squad.

After earning All-America honors as a hard-hitting linebacker, Lynch starred for the Kansas City Chiefs for 11 seasons. A perennial All-Pro in the NFL and a member of the Chiefs' ring of honor, Lynch considers being Notre Dame's captain his greatest honor in sports.

Today, Lynch is president of D. Thomas and Associates, a Kansas City food-packaging company he started after completing law school and deciding to raise his family in the Midwest. He and his wife, Georgia, have three children and five grandchildren.

Their two daughters, Megan and Kara, are Notre Dame graduates—"kind of funny for a guy who was at Notre Dame at the time of 'better dead than coed,'" Lynch laughs. The couple's son Jake graduated from Regis University in Denver.

Along with his family and business, Lynch finds time to contribute to Notre Dame. Lynch has served as the president of Notre Dame's National Monogram Club and occasionally is called upon to provide informal counsel and guidance.

"Being a part of Notre Dame was great, and anything I can do, I'm happy to do it," he says.

"Without wearing it on your sleeve, Notre Dame's Catholic identity is what makes it special," Lynch offers.

"Obviously, if you're accepted into Notre Dame, you've been given a lot of talent, but Notre Dame teaches you that there is more to life than profit and loss. You have a duty to learn, but you also have a duty to share."

Catching Up with...George Goeddeke

George Goeddeke was usually right in the middle of everything.

As the All-American center on Notre Dame's 1966 national championship team, that was to be expected. But outside the lines, Goeddeke defied the stereotype of offensive linemen as being serious. Stories abound of Goeddeke's off-the-field adventures.

"I was very uninhibited," Goeddeke admits.

In some ways, Goeddeke's antics off the field were just as important to Notre Dame's success as his all-star performance on the field. Notre Dame coach Ara Parseghian was known as a tough taskmaster who fielded well-prepared teams. Even so, Parseghian saw fit to cut Goeddeke and his teammates some slack.

"We would run through walls for Ara," says Goeddeke. "While we were on the field, we played disciplined football. Having a little fun off the field helped provide a release for some of that pressure, and I think Ara understood that."

Every once in a while, Goeddeke found himself the victim of some hijinks. One example illustrated how his brand of leadership helped build a cohesive football team.

"One night before a game we were at Moreau Seminary," recalls Goeddeke. "After the team watched a movie, those of us who imbibed in nicotine would sneak up onto the roof for a cigarette.

"I got back to my room to go to sleep and Terry Hanratty jumped out of the closet. I just about jumped out of my skin," Goeddeke laughs.

Hanratty, of course, was the sophomore star quarterback on the '66 team. He and his classmate Jim Seymour received the lion's share of publicity on that team, including a cover shot for *Time* magazine.

The situation could have been a disaster, but not to Goeddeke's way of thinking.

"We all trusted Ara," he explains. "If these guys were going to take us to the promised land, that was fine with us."

Goeddeke later played six seasons with the NFL's Denver Broncos. Since then, he's made his home near Detroit with his wife, Geneva. The couple, married for more than 35 years, has five adult children and a grade-school-aged son—a "bonus baby" as Goeddeke puts it. "He keeps us on our toes," Goeddeke laughs.

"God has been very good to us and we thank Him every day," he said.

From Gridiron to Supreme Court:
Page and Thomas Still Making a Difference

"Some would say the problems are too big and too complex for one person to impact. I believe those people are wrong. You don't need to be a Supreme Court justice or even a football hero to make change happen. Everyone here, and I emphasize everyone, has the ability, the opportunity, and I believe the obligation to make this world a better place." —Justice Alan Page, Notre Dame Commencement Address, May 16, 2004

"As lawyers and judges, we must remember one essential fact: at the heart of every case is a human being—a person for whom this particular case means everything." —Chief Justice Robert Thomas, First Remarks as Chief Justice, September 7, 2005

May I please the Court?

Ladies and gentlemen of the Notre Dame community, I thank you for allowing me to share my time with you this afternoon, but I can assure you that your work here represents the most important of civic duties. I now have the opportunity to present to you an opening statement, which is a preview of what the evidence will show during this hearing.

Over the course of the next several minutes you will begin to hear the story of two distinguished Notre Dame individuals—Justice Alan Page of the Minnesota Supreme Court and Chief Justice Robert Thomas of the Illinois Supreme Court.

The similarities appear remarkable. Both share the same birthday (August 7), instrumental roles as seniors on national championship teams (1966 and 1973), and professional football career paths that crossed for four seasons in Chicago (1978 through 1981).

A three-year starter at defensive end for Notre Dame, Alan Page was a consensus All-American in 1966 for the Irish. He went on to play 15 seasons in the NFL with Minnesota and Chicago, playing in four Super Bowls.

But I implore you to look beyond these mere coincidences.

Minnesota Supreme Court justice and former Fighting Irish and NFL star Alan Page gives a Notre Dame commencement address on May 16, 2004. Photo courtesy of AP/Wide World Photos.

The differences seem overwhelming. Both maintain different political affiliations (Democrat and Republican), skin color (black and white), and reputations as football standouts (the most feared member of the Purple People Eaters and a kicker whose only contact came with his right leg, the football, and the netting behind the goal posts).

I ask you again to ignore these superficial discrepancies.

Rather, this case is about the meaning of a vocation. The evidence will show that the careers of Justices Page and Thomas exemplify this notion and convey a lifetime example for all to follow.

Opposing counsel will have you think otherwise. "But for football, where would these men be?" "Is there a place for faith in public life?" "Can one person make a difference?" Each is a valid question to be raised at trial, but each can be answered.

And it is in response to these questions that the case for each justice begins to unfold at Notre Dame and, perhaps ironically, with former head coach Ara Parseghian, who is more associated with a locker room than a courtroom but whose impact looms large nonetheless.

Then a freshman from Canton, Ohio, and still following the footsteps of an older brother, Page learned from Parseghian a philosophy on life before he ever defended one snap on the college gridiron.

At a team meeting in the spring of 1964, Parseghian spoke of football as a game defined solely by field position and possession. Page understood the message for its profound symbolism.

"It was one of those eye-opening moments where I learned there was a theory and philosophy to football," says Page. "What Ara was really saying is that if you do all the things that are necessary to maintain field position and possession, such as avoiding penalties and mistakes, you will be successful. In the practice of law and in relationships with others, if we understand the big picture and take care of little things, we stand a good chance of being successful."

Page would ultimately make a career of helping others stand a good chance of being successful in their own right. An explanation of the way in which he does this is best coupled with an understanding of the journey of Justice Thomas.

Then a senior reeling from a slow start to his final collegiate season, Thomas learned from Parseghian a lesson in the importance of confidence.

"Right before the USC game, Ara walked off the practice field with me and told me that he didn't need me in the other games, but that he would need me on Saturday," says Thomas. "I had three field goals that day, and we won by nine points."

No kick, however, was bigger than his 19-yard field goal in the closing moments of the 1973 Sugar Bowl to deliver a national championship with a 24–23 victory against Alabama.

Yet, Thomas's impact extends far beyond the ball that made its way over the crossbar and inside the right upright on that memorable New Year's Eve in New Orleans.

Thomas experienced a 12-year professional football career, in which he played 10 seasons with the Chicago Bears and still ranks as team record-holder for field goals and points scored by a kicker. While playing professional football, he earned his J.D. from Loyola University School of Law in 1981.

After seven years of practice in civil litigation, Thomas was elected to the state circuit court in 1988 and to the state appellate court six years later. Thomas earned a seat on Illinois's highest court with election to the Supreme Court in 2000—and eventually was sworn in as Chief Justice.

"When I thought about being a judge, someone asked me how I would handle lawyers in the courtroom," says Thomas. "Being booed by 80,000 people as a player, I replied that I didn't know why anyone should worry."

Thomas has yet to be booed in the courtroom, although he admits that some counsel have come dangerously close.

It is just a coincidence, however, that in his first remarks as chief justice, Thomas spoke of the need for collegiality and professional civility in the legal profession—a primary goal since his first days on the Court. The Illinois Supreme Court soon after approved new rules designed to improve the quality of legal services and promote civility among lawyers. The initiatives require the establishment of a permanent commission on professionalism.

Illinois Supreme Court justice Bob Thomas speaks inside the Illinois Supreme Courthouse on September 14, 2005. Like Alan Page, with whom he played on the Chicago Bears for four years, Thomas won a national championship at Notre Dame. Photo courtesy of AP/Wide World Photos.

As important as civility is to Thomas in the profession, he quotes scripture in that same speech, speaking of his faith, acting justly, and walking humbly.

"My faith is very important to me," says Thomas. "I have been blessed with two great careers. Knowing that self-esteem is not based on what you do but rather that you are a child of God becomes the most important factor in my personal life."

While faith in part drives Thomas personally and professionally, a similar conviction inspires Page.

Page sparked the Irish to their first national championship in 17 seasons as a consensus All-American in 1966. A first-round selection of the Minnesota Vikings, Page's professional football career spanned 15 seasons and four Super Bowls. He earned four conference Defensive Player of the Year honors and became the first defensive player in league history to win the league's Most Valuable Player award. Page was inducted into both the Professional and College Football Halls of Fame.

Receiving a J.D. from the University of Minnesota in 1978, Page began private practice in Minnesota a year later. He became an assistant attorney general for Minnesota in 1987, where he concentrated on employment litigation. Page was elected to the Minnesota Supreme Court in 1992 and was reelected in 1998 and again in 2004.

"Both my Notre Dame background and my professional football background have provided the opportunity for me to get heard in the first instance," says Page. "After that, you have to have something worth talking about so people will listen."

His message speaks volumes for the cause of educating the less fortunate.

From the steps of the Hall of Fame at his induction speech in Canton in 1988, Page started the Page Education Foundation to provide educational grants to students of color to attend college in Minnesota. Today, the foundation has awarded nearly $5 million of aid to more than 2,000 students.

His off-the-field contributions prompted the NCAA in January 2004 to present him with its Theodore Roosevelt Award, one of the NCAA's two highest awards, at its annual convention in Nashville, Tennessee. Page's journey came full circle when he delivered the commencement address at the 2004 Notre Dame commencement ceremonies with Page scholar Andrea Manka graduating from the university that same day.

"Each of us in our own small way can make big changes," says Page. "Whether it is related to issues of character or beginning to solve what seems to be the problem with respect to race, we have the ability to bring about change through our efforts. We can take responsibility for what we do and say, and can look inward to see what our role is and how we can change what we do."

The jurisprudence of Justices Page and Thomas will reflect integrity and just application of law to facts.

Their voices will echo social change and faith.

Their actions will demonstrate character and conviction.

The evidence will show that every person has the obligation to make the world a better place and at the heart of every case is a human being. This verdict should be on the side of vocations.

Catching Up with...Bob Gladieux

Bob Gladieux was one of Notre Dame's biggest heroes in one of the biggest games in Notre Dame football history. Although he led Notre Dame's 1968 team in rushing and scoring, Gladieux probably is best remembered for scoring the only Irish touchdown in the legendary 10–10 tie against Michigan State in 1966.

Notre Dame rallied from a 10–0 deficit against the Spartans largely due to its ability to make adjustments, especially with injuries. Several Irish stars missed all or much of the game. Others played with serious injuries.

It's a good thing for Gladieux that he absorbed that lesson about making adjustments. More than 20 years later, Gladieux was back at Notre Dame, obtaining his master's degree and serving as a graduate assistant under Irish head coach Lou Holtz.

When it came time to leave Notre Dame for a second time, Gladieux had more than a degree and two years at the knee of one of the all-time coaching greats—he also had a new partner.

While Gladieux was completing his master's degree, a friend attempted to arrange a blind date for the former Irish star. According to Gladieux, while he was all for the idea, his prospective date, a native of Germany who was working for a South Bend travel company, wasn't interested.

"She said, 'Football player? Fat neck. No brains. No thanks,'" Gladieux relates, before adding with a laugh, "But then she met me."

Gladieux married Inge, who has traveled to more than 180 countries and speaks five languages. As Gladieux puts it, "She's the franchise."

Gladieux recognized that the situation called for an adjustment. Instead of moving on to the next destination in his coaching career, Bob and Inge started Gladieux Travel, Inc., in South Bend, serving individuals and businesses since 1988. More recently, Bob has also become associated with Za-Meks, a provider of clocks, mirrors, and other promotional items. Za-Meks is licensed with Notre Dame and more than 40 other universities.

Raising daughters Annette, Anja, and Molly, Gladieux has made yet another adjustment.

"I didn't have any sisters—this has been different. We had a blast until they became teenagers," he laughs.

Gladieux stays close to the Notre Dame program, attending away games along with tours offered by Gladieux Travel.

"These players are great kids," he said, "and I always congratulate them on the commitment they've made by coming to Notre Dame."

Catching Up with…Coley O'Brien

Coley O'Brien made the first start of his Notre Dame career in the final game of his sophomore season, one week after replacing injured classmate Terry Hanratty at quarterback in Notre Dame's fabled 10–10 tie with Michigan State.

In that season finale, O'Brien completed 21 of 31 passes for 255 yards and three touchdowns as the Irish pummeled 10th-ranked Southern California 51–0 to cement their number one ranking.

But O'Brien and everyone else knew that the starting job in 1967 would belong to Hanratty, who finished eighth in the 1966 Heisman Trophy balloting. Today's "experts" would speculate that, blocked on the Notre Dame depth chart, O'Brien would transfer in search of playing time, stardom, and ESPN highlight clips.

But O'Brien didn't switch schools; he switched positions, becoming a halfback in Irish head coach Ara Parseghian's full-house backfield. According to longtime Irish offensive coordinator Tom Pagna, O'Brien was the best blocking back he ever coached.

"Football was my entry into Notre Dame," explains O'Brien. "It was a dream come true to be able to attend Notre Dame, and it didn't enter my mind about moving to another school."

O'Brien helped the Irish to a 24–4–2 record during his three years on the varsity before earning his law degree from Notre Dame. The McLean, Virginia, native returned home, earning a reputation as one of Capitol Hill's most effective lobbyists. O'Brien currently leads NASA's legislative efforts, helping to promote the agency's vision and program for space exploration in Congress.

"It's very exciting to be working as part of NASA's space exploration program," says O'Brien, who inherited his fascination with space travel from his father, a graduate of the U.S. Naval Academy. O'Brien has passed his love for Notre Dame on to his three children—Christin (an '06 Notre Dame graduate), Conor, and Cara.

"With Ara, every time we took the field, we knew that if we executed properly, he and the coaches had given us the schemes we would need to win the game—no matter who our opponent was," remembers O'Brien.

Of course, of particular interest to O'Brien has been the play of Irish quarterback Brady Quinn.

"If I were being recruited as a quarterback today, I'd say, 'I think Charlie is the guy.'"

Catching Up with...Mr. Fling (Terry Hanratty) and Mr. Cling (Jim Seymour)

Neither the passage of time nor hundreds of miles have disrupted the rhythm and timing of Terry Hanratty and Jim Seymour.

It has been over 40 years since the duo made their spectacular debut against Purdue in Notre Dame Stadium. Widely acclaimed as the missing ingredients in a Notre Dame team destined for glory, the two sophomores more than lived up to their billing.

Seymour caught 13 of Hanratty's passes as the Irish pounded eighth-ranked Purdue 26–14. His 276 receiving yards still stand as a Notre Dame single-game record.

By November the undefeated Irish were atop the national polls. Hanratty and Seymour, nicknamed "Fling" and "Cling" by Notre Dame rookie sports information director Roger Valdiserri, were on the cover of *Time* magazine.

The pair was tremendously gifted, but both men worked hard for their great success. Between the practice fields and the fieldhouse, Hanratty threw thousands of passes to Seymour. By the time they debuted against the Boilermakers, Seymour knew exactly when to break off his route and Hanratty knew exactly when to let fly.

Today, Hanratty can start a sentence, only to have Seymour finish it for him without missing a beat. Each recalls feeling pretty good about the season-opening win over the Boilermakers, until the Irish coaching staff critiqued the game film.

"Sunday night..." remembers Hanratty.

"We found out just how many mistakes we made in that game," interjects Seymour.

"We came out of that film room feeling like we had lost the game," laughs Hanratty.

Not only did the Irish not lose that day, but they didn't lose at all in 1966, clinching the national championship with a season-ending 51–0 annihilation of Southern California.

Both players sing the same tune when it comes to giving credit for their accomplishments and the team's gaudy record. Each point to Irish head coach Ara Parseghian as the most important factor in that success.

"Ara let us be us," explains Hanratty.

Seymour agrees. "And Ara had a great staff," he says.

"Ara stressed preparation," elaborates Hanratty. "We were never surprised by anything that happened in a game."

"The games were actually a relief," claims Seymour. "We were practicing against the best defense in the country all year. Johnny Ray, our defensive coordinator, hated it when anybody made his defense look bad, even in practice. And we weren't able to do that very often."

The duo may not have made Ray's pride and joy look bad too often in practice, but Hanratty and Seymour made plenty of opposing defenses look sick.

At the close of their three-year careers (under NCAA rules, freshmen were ineligible to play in those days), Seymour and Hanratty owned a host of Notre Dame records. In addition to his single-game records for receptions and receiving yards, Seymour graduated with the most receptions in Notre Dame history (138 for 2,113 yards). Hanratty graduated as Notre Dame's all-time leader in passing and total offense.

Hanratty finished in the top 10 in the Heisman Trophy balloting at the close of each of his three seasons, capped by a third-place finish as a senior in 1968. Both players received first-team All-America recognition during their final season at Notre Dame.

Both played for several years in the NFL before retiring and entering private business. Seymour established an insurance business in the Chicago area. Meanwhile, Hanratty has found that the ability to make split-second decisions as a college and professional quarterback is serving him well as a stock trader.

Recent years have seen Seymour's son (one of three) and Hanratty's daughter (one of four) in the same Notre Dame graduating class. Seymour is now involving his children in his insurance business and enjoying his grandchildren.

"Jimmy retired and I started another family," jokes Hanratty in reference to his grade-school-age son and daughter to go with three adult daughters.

Coaching has kept Hanratty away from Notre Dame Stadium for the past few seasons, while Seymour is a regular fixture.

Nonetheless, they both still see the same things when they watch the game.

"Nobody throws the ball deep anymore," laments Hanratty. "And if I were playing today, I'd never use a huddle..."

"So the defense wouldn't be able to substitute the way they do," explains Seymour.

"Exactly," agrees Hanratty.

And just like that, it's Hanratty to Seymour all over again.

Catching Up with...Mike McCoy

At 6'5" and 270 pounds, Mike McCoy couldn't help but have a large impact.

McCoy was so good at making his presence felt that he became a unanimous first-team All-American defensive tackle at Notre Dame and an 11-year star in the NFL.

Now, more than 20 years after retiring from football, McCoy is dedicated to having an even greater impact on young people around the world. McCoy is the national director of Champions for Today (www.championsfortoday.org), a group of former NFL players and athletes committed to speaking to young people to help them make positive life choices and changes.

A few years after retiring from the NFL, McCoy was jolted by a conversation with his adolescent daughter in which she spoke to him about the pressure on young teens to engage in sexual activity and experiment with drugs and alcohol.

"It just kind of hit me," McCoy remembers. "I asked myself how I could use the platform that I have from playing at Notre Dame and in the NFL to make a dent in society."

Having been involved with Fellowship of Christian Athletes during his days with the Green Bay Packers, McCoy joined a number of other former NFL players with Bill Glass Ministries.

The father of four and a grandfather of three—"I'm still in denial about being a grandparent," McCoy jokes—it is clear that while McCoy speaks to a wide variety of groups, his greatest passion is the youth.

"Every young person in the country is at risk today because of our culture," says McCoy. "We try to help them understand that they are made in the image of Jesus Christ and that he's there to help them."

Catching Up with…Walt Patulski

When Walt Patulski looked around upon arriving at Notre Dame, he noticed lots of guys just like himself—big, strong, and talented.

"There was so much amazing talent at Notre Dame," recalls Patulski. "The abilities are pretty equal. You would see some guys not being able to translate those skills into effective play and others with marginal talent accomplishing a lot through great effort and mind-set. That's what I was interested in studying."

Patulski did not come to Notre Dame as a defensive end or as a defensive player. He was a standout fullback at Christian

Brothers Academy in Liverpool, New York (a suburb of Syracuse), where he won nine letters in football, basketball, and track. Tempted to follow in the footsteps of fullback Larry Csonka at Syracuse, Patulski opted instead for South Bend.

Moved from fullback to defensive end less than a week into his freshman season, Patulski found a way to rise to the top amid all the talent. By the time he was a senior, Patulski, who started every game of his Notre Dame career, was the UPI's Lineman of the Year, finishing ninth in the Heisman Trophy ballotting and winning the Lombardi Trophy as the country's best lineman.

Despite the acclaim he won from the media and the public, Patulski ranks being elected by his teammates as Notre Dame's captain for his senior season as the biggest thrill of his college career.

"Being recognized by your colleagues as being worthy of leading them was quite an honor," says Patulski, who was the number one pick in the entire 1972 NFL draft by the Buffalo Bills.

After injuries cut short Patulski's professional career (four years with Buffalo and one with St. Louis), he established himself in the financial services profession. More recently, he has also begun to share the insights he gleaned from watching football players battle to rise to the top of the depth chart.

Patulski's audio series, "Vitamins and Minerals for the Mind," examines keys to success in all aspects of life. In helping others learn how to get the most out of their natural gifts, Patulski is simply following his own advice.

"Without a doubt, you have to do something you have a passion for," he says. "And this is my passion."

Catching Up with...Roger Valdiserri

Want to start a fight?

Nominate somebody as the best ever in his chosen endeavor.

Except when it comes to Roger Valdiserri. Notre Dame's former sports information director is universally regarded as the best ever at his profession. A 1954 graduate of Notre Dame, Valdiserri spent nearly 30 years overseeing sports publicity at his alma mater.

Valdiserri not only survived change, he created it.

"That was the beautiful thing about stepping into the job; there were a lot of opportunities to try new things," recalls Valdiserri.

Long before teleconferences and modern technologies, Valdiserri had Irish head football coach Ara Parseghian record answers to questions for the media. The system dramatically reduced the time that Parseghian had to spend meeting enormous media demands.

For nearly three decades, Valdiserri masterfully negotiated a tightrope between providing the media with desired information and access and helping the coaches and players cooperate without becoming overwhelmed or distracted.

"It all goes back to how willing a coach is to make some adjustments for the good of the program and the university," he says. "And they've all been great."

Valdiserri may be best known for the changing of Joe Theismann's name from THEES-man to THEIS-man—which happened to rhyme with *Heisman*.

Great is an appropriate word to describe Valdiserri's contributions to Notre Dame. He's a member of the College Sports Information Directors of America (CoSIDA) Hall of Fame and was named one of the 100 most influential people in college football.

"Working with Roger was like following the Pied Piper," says John Heisler, who came to work for Valdiserri in 1978 as Notre Dame's assistant sports information director and followed Valdiserri into the CoSIDA Hall of Fame. "When it came to athletics, there wasn't anyone he didn't know. If you rode around on his coattails, you met everyone in the business."

Today, Valdiserri plays the Pied Piper to his seven grandchildren. He recently returned to South Bend, building a new home to allow him to spend more time with his five children—all Notre Dame graduates—and those grandchildren.

Yesterday's Heroes: Clarence Ellis

"Notre Dame fans should feel happy that Ellis is Ellis. He's the type who some underprivileged kid will probably pattern himself after some day. That's Clarence Ellis. That's the kind of person he is." —*South Bend Tribune*, 1970

And that's exactly what happened.

On the gridiron, Clarence Ellis seemed to always face a challenge that he would eventually overcome.

Offered an athletic football scholarship by only Notre Dame and Western Michigan, Ellis turned the notion that he was too small to compete into pure nonsense. In so doing, he became a three-year starter in the Notre Dame secondary, a consensus All-America pick in 1971, and the 15th overall selection of the 1972 NFL draft. Ellis played professionally for three seasons with the Atlanta Falcons before retiring from the Denver Broncos in 1975 and embarking on a successful career with the IBM Corporation, Honeywell International, and finally the Dekalb County School District in suburban Atlanta.

But his most lasting accomplishment may very well be the manner in which he enabled others to overcome challenges in their lives.

James Easton, a husband and father of three, provides proof of this legacy.

"I get choked up when I talk about Clarence," says Easton, who notes that only his mother and Ellis refer to him as Jimmy. "The way Clarence did things was a good example for me in my life. I would not be who I am right now without him."

Easton's parents divorced when he was six years old. Without a male figure for Easton to look toward for support, his mother turned to the Big Brothers Big Sisters program of South Bend and, ultimately, Ellis.

Ellis provided much more than support, counseling Easton on both academics and life lessons throughout Easton's adolescent years. In his first year in the professional ranks, Ellis funded the round-trip airfare for Easton and his brother to attend a Falcons game and visit with Ellis and his teammates. The relationship has since lasted a lifetime.

Easton would go on the play college basketball at Mississippi Valley State. Today, he coaches and teaches in Jacksonville—a career vocation he attributes to Ellis—and dreams of the day that his children will be able to attend Notre Dame.

"Clarence always told me that you can't cry about spilled milk," says Easton. "You can't put it back in the bottle. Just go forward."

Such a philosophy suits Ellis well. After playing his last game for the Falcons, Ellis waited two decades before attending another. Nearly as much time passed before he returned to campus for a game after his graduation in 1972, but Ellis made the trip to watch his nephew march in the band.

Yet, Ellis would only let a few months transpire without keeping in touch with Easton.

"Life gets to a point where you get down to basics—family and those individuals who are close and dear to you," says Ellis, who admittedly is echoing his former coach Ara Parseghian's advice regarding appreciating opportunities in the moment.

"With so much going on, you kind of realize that things can be swept away very quickly," he said. "Nothing is guaranteed. Right now I am just trying to keep it simple."

Ellis keeps it simple today—he takes breaks from the Fayetteville, Arkansas, heat to visit his grandchildren in Grand Rapids, North Dakota, and enjoys each day with his wife, Renee, whom Ellis identifies as his life's passion.

And he has never forgotten the basics. Just ask Jimmy.

Catching Up with...Tom Gatewood

Amid the fact-filled Notre Dame football media guide, even an All-American can become a footnote to history. A two-time All-American and the former holder of Notre Dame's single-season record for receptions (77 in 1970), Tom Gatewood is determined to prevent that from happening to him.

Realizing that he has more to offer than faded newspaper clippings, Gatewood jumped at the opportunity to become involved with a committee charged with trying to find NCAA-approved ways for former Irish football players to become involved in the current program.

One way Gatewood does that is with visits to Notre Dame practices.

"Being on the practice field and demonstrating tips for the players was almost as if I had come out of a cartoon or as if I had come off of the pages of a book," relates Gatewood.

Sometimes, Gatewood provides his own résumé.

"I like to show footage—no more than two or three minutes," he says. "Then the players can see that even though I'm gray and wrinkled, in my day, I could do what they do."

Gatewood's list of accomplishments didn't end when he graduated from Notre Dame. Blue Atlas Productions, an ad specialty company owned by Gatewood, numbers American Express, Merrill Lynch, and NBC among its clients. Gatewood's video/television production company, Larkspur Lane Ltd., has an Emmy to its credit.

"It's good for players to see those things," Gatewood says. "But they also need to hear that before you get to this point, you've got to do what you're doing right now and you've got to do it well."

Notre Dame surely would be well-served were Gatewood to become a role model for current players.

Gatewood attributes much of his success at Notre Dame to Irish coach Ara Parseghian and quarterback Joe Theismann. Rather than national awards, Gatewood speaks with pride of being elected by his Irish teammates captain both of the freshman team and later the varsity squad.

To Gatewood, a three-touchdown performance against Army in Yankee Stadium is noteworthy because of how much his parents—who had never seen him play football before—enjoyed the experience.

Having already made his own history, Gatewood is trying to help players make their own history—on and off the field.

Catching Up with...Greg Marx

Mother knows best?

As a highly recruited high school football player, Greg Marx had narrowed his choice of colleges to three, and Notre Dame was not on the list. Shortly before signing day, he sought his mother's input.

"'Sit on the couch, I want to tell you a story,'" Marx recalls his mother saying. Marx's mother told of how her family had come to Michigan from Canada, lured by the opportunity to earn five dollars per day in Henry Ford's auto plants.

After World War II started, Marx's mother worked on the assembly line. As many Americans did, she bought war bonds. Beyond supporting the U.S. military, Marx's mother had a secondary motive in purchasing the bonds.

"She told me that if she ever had a son, and he wanted to go to Notre Dame, she would be able to afford to send him," relates Marx. That was all Marx needed to hear. And thanks to Marx's football talent, his mother didn't need to cash in those war bonds to see her dream come true.

As a sophomore (freshmen were ineligible for the varsity), Marx earned a starting position at defensive tackle, only to break his forearm in the final preseason scrimmage. Marx came back to win the starting position for 1970 and 1971.

After the 1971 season, Irish head coach Ara Parseghian summoned Marx to his office. "He told me that the team had voted me as one of the captains, but before he announced it, he wanted to make sure I was coming back, because some NFL teams had expressed interest in me."

A three-year starter at defensive tackle, Greg Marx served as cocaptain of the 1972 Notre Dame football team that was 8–3 and played in the 1973 Orange Bowl against Nebraska.

"I told Ara that if they want me back, I'm in," he said.

Marx capped his Notre Dame career by earning unanimous All-America honors and two postgraduate scholarships. He was selected in the second round of the NFL draft by the Atlanta Falcons before injuries cut short his football career after one season.

He went on to earn his degree from the Notre Dame Law School in 1977, putting his law degree to work in both the banking and the securities industries. Marx jokes that he recently enjoyed a big pay raise, as the youngest of his four children graduated from college.

"I spent 16 consecutive years putting someone through college," he laughs.

The children—Aaron, Jason, Megan, and Maureen—are scattered around the country, and Aaron has done two tours of duty in Iraq as a Marine Corps major, piloting attack planes. Marx still remains close to them, a priority he no doubt learned from his mother, who, without a driver's license, rode buses to show up at the door of Marx's dorm room the morning after he broke his forearm as a freshman.

And what of her role in Marx's decision to attend Notre Dame?

"There is a spirit at Notre Dame," Marx says. "It really is a special place."

Indeed, Mother does know best.

Irish Football 1973:
Changes Bring About a Championship

If 24-hour radio talk shows and all-sports television networks had been in existence on January 1, 1973, could you imagine the intonations of the talking heads as the clock approached midnight and Nebraska was celebrating its 40–6 thrashing of Notre Dame in the Orange Bowl?

Announcer 1: Coming on the heels of Notre Dame's 45–23 loss to Southern California in its final regular-season game, this loss really raises some questions about the direction of the Irish program.

Announcer 2: I agree. First, Anthony Davis scores six touchdowns for USC against Notre Dame, and now Johnny Rodgers scores four tonight for the Cornhuskers. Notre Dame barely managed 200 yards of total offense, while surrendering 560 yards of total offense to Nebraska. Maybe Ara Parseghian used smoke and mirrors to win that national championship in 1966 and to lead the Irish to top-10 finishes in each of his first seven seasons at Notre Dame. This marks the first time Notre Dame has lost three games in a season since 1963. I think perhaps the game has passed Parseghian by a little bit.

In his book, *Era of Ara*, coauthored with Bob Best, longtime Parseghian assistant coach Tom Pagna described the three defeats suffered by the '72 team, which included a 30–26 upset loss to Missouri in October, as "three of the most stunning defeats in Notre Dame history."

But if people doubted Parseghian's ability to once again produce teams that lived up to the lofty standards he had established for himself at Notre Dame, they did so at their own peril. Parseghian, whose intensity was legendary, challenged his players and his staff—and most of all, himself—as never before.

Pagna remembers Parseghian's drive in the weeks and months following the Orange Bowl: "Ara was constantly asking the staff, 'Where did we go wrong? What mistakes did we make as coaches?'"

During the off-season, Notre Dame switched from its customary 4-4-3 defense to a 4-3-4 alignment. Starting positions were up for grabs. No fewer than four returning starters from the '72 team found themselves in backup roles

And Parseghian implemented new team rules.

"Ara had always been one to listen to the players," recalls Pagna. "When assistants would argue that we should have restrictions on the length of players' hair and things like that, Ara would always say, 'Give me something I can hang my hat on. Give me a reason to do it.'

"And if we couldn't provide an adequate rationale for a rule like that, Ara wouldn't go for it. He didn't always agree with a lot of what was going on in those days, but he wouldn't impose rules without having a legitimate reason.

"But after the '72 season, he decided that we were going to put some new rules into place, and for the first time, we really clamped down. And he really stuck with it."

New players, rules, and formations? Some would see these as desperate moves by a captain ready to go down with his ship.

But not this time.

If it would be difficult to imagine a more disheartening start to 1973 than Notre Dame's performance in the Orange Bowl on January 1, 1973, it would be even more difficult to imagine a more spectacular and satisfying conclusion to 1973 than the Irish provided with their performance in the Sugar Bowl on the night of December 31, 1973.

Parseghian's team needed only 364 days to completely vindicate itself, as the Irish completed Notre Dame's first perfect season since 1949 and earned Notre Dame's ninth consensus national championship with an electrifying 24–23 upset of top-ranked Alabama.

Even Parseghian was surprised to be sitting atop the college football world quite so soon.

"It was unexpected," Parseghian confesses. "I thought we were a year away."

Everybody connected with the '73 Irish agrees that team chemistry was critical to the team's success. But debating who is most responsible for creating that chemistry makes for some lively conversation.

To a man, the players point to their coach. Parseghian points right back at them, praising both talent and attitude.

Parseghian, when pressed for a key to the '73 season, points to the unexpected contributions from prize freshmen Ross Browner, Luther Bradley, Al Hunter, and Willie Fry.

"The thing that stands out in my mind was the ability of our freshmen to make big contributions in the areas where we needed them most," he says.

"They fit in as if they were perfect pieces to a puzzle.

Ara Parseghian leads his team onto the field for Media Day in August 1973, setting the mood for that season's national championship. Photo courtesy of AP/Wide World Photos.

"Sometimes it takes two or three years before a player is ready to step in and contribute. How lucky can you be?"

Pagna is having none of that.

"He is a born leader," says Pagna of Parseghian.

"He has that rare, rare ability to focus and pinpoint exactly what are the key points to success, and to communicate them to the team."

Pagna, who played for Parseghian at Miami of Ohio and coached with him at both Northwestern and Notre Dame, also credits the leadership of Notre Dame's captains—seniors Dave Casper, Mike Townsend, and Frank Pomarico—along with junior quarterback Tom Clements and junior linebacker Greg Collins.

Parseghian also praises the leadership provided by the older players, many of whom lost playing time upon the arrival of the fabulous freshmen.

"Sometimes it's tough between the groups of younger players and older players," acknowledges Parseghian. "But we had excellent chemistry."

Parseghian had a well-deserved reputation for being an exacting taskmaster, but he went out of his way to make sure his players also had fun. The delight in his voice is still unmistakable as he recounts the intrasquad "talent" competitions held at the close of practice each Thursday.

"The offense would come up with some jingle about our upcoming opponent, something about how we'd kick their tails," explains Parseghian. "Then the defense would take its turn, singing a jingle. And then the scout team would perform one. They'd all be cheering like hell, looking at me to pronounce the winner. I'd take my time, pretending that I was really trying to decide. I'd finally announce a winner, and they acted like they'd just won the Super Bowl.

"That was something, to see that kind of exuberance at the end of practice," Parseghian says. "It was important to know that we would work hard, but that we'd also have fun.

"After all these years, I still tell my wife I wish we had gotten some of those talent shows on film."

At least there is plenty of film capturing the on-the-field exploits of the Irish.

As Parseghian's young team was finding its way early in the season, it faced a stern midseason test in USC. Notre Dame hadn't defeated the Trojans since 1966, but the Irish proved they were for real with a 23–14 win over the sixth-ranked Trojans.

Bradley set the stage on the first play from scrimmage. The rookie defensive back hit USC star flanker Lynn Swann so hard that he not only broke up quarterback Pat Haden's pass, but also knocked Swann's helmet completely off his head.

Junior halfback Eric Penick broke the Trojans' backs in the third quarter, exploding through a gaping hole opened by the left side of the Notre Dame line to race 85 yards down the sideline for a touchdown. Nobody touched Penick until he was mobbed in the end zone by the Notre Dame student section.

Although undefeated, the Irish were only ranked third when they took the field against top-ranked Alabama in the Sugar Bowl.

Somehow, the first-ever meeting between the legendary programs and their legendary coaches—Parseghian and the Crimson Tide's Paul "Bear" Bryant—managed to live up to its incredible pregame buildup. The lead changed hands six times, with Irish kicker Bob Thomas's 19-yard field goal with 4:26 to play providing Notre Dame's 24–23 margin of victory.

But the matter wasn't settled until Sugar Bowl MVP Clements completed a third-down pass from his own end zone to tight end Robin Weber, allowing Notre Dame to run out the clock.

Can you hear the talk-radio hosts and the all-sports stations now?

Announcer 1: Notre Dame proved tonight why it is always one of the top teams in the country.

Announcer 2: Ara Parseghian proved tonight that he is a true genius among college coaches.

Bookstore Legends

If you've ever wondered how athletic you have to be to play quarterback at Notre Dame, check out the results of Bookstore Basketball, Notre Dame's spring outdoor single-elimination basketball tournament that features more than 500 teams that play in any weather. The game winner is the first team to 21 by one.

Bookstore began in 1972, and a year later Irish signal-caller Tom Clements won his first title, followed by another in '75 (Clements was MVP of the event that second year). Joe Montana's team won the '77 crown, and Rusty Lisch helped his team to the championship game all four years he played, including titles in '78, '79, and '80. Steve Beuerlein claimed a runner-up finish in '84 and a first-place trophy in '86. Tony Rice played on teams that finished second in '89 and '90. Brady Quinn's team won the title in 2006 (though he didn't play in the finale).

Catching Up with...Mike Townsend

It only seems appropriate that Notre Dame had to come up with an "interception" of its own in order to land the player who still holds the Irish record for interceptions in a single season.

Unlike his older brother Willie, Mike Townsend did not grow up dreaming of playing football at Notre Dame. So while Willie was learning his way as a freshman on the Irish squad during the 1968–1969 season, Mike was a high school senior entertaining offers from dozens of colleges.

After deciding to attend Purdue, Mike returned home from school to find Irish assistant coach Brian Boulac, much to his surprise. Somehow, Boulac had learned of Mike's decision and had decided to pay a visit—completely legitimate under NCAA rules at the time. Boulac spent a couple of hours "recruiting" Mrs. Townsend while awaiting Mike's arrival.

Mike's mom was convinced that Notre Dame was the place for him but remained true to the promise she had made along with Mike's father to leave the decision to Mike. A little while later, Mike's girlfriend arrived—presumably not orchestrated by Boulac—and told Mike that he should go to Notre Dame.

Mike hadn't previously involved his girlfriend in the decision-making process, but once he did, she decided that an all-male school was definitely the place for Mike. (No, Mike didn't tell her about the proximity of Saint Mary's College to Notre Dame; and no, Mike did not eventually marry the young woman.)

The rest, as they say, is history—literally. As a junior, Townsend led the nation with his 10 interceptions. Townsend's 13 career interceptions rank third on the all-time Notre Dame list. In 1973 he earned consensus All-America honors to help lead Notre Dame to a national championship. Not only was Mike reunited with big brother Willie on the football field, but the pair also played varsity basketball.

After retiring from professional football, Townsend returned to Ohio, where for more than 20 years he has worked for the U.S. Department of Energy. Townsend has five children, including a son who played varsity basketball at Tennessee–Chattanooga, and another who studied engineering at Duke. Townsend still lives with his wife and three other children in his hometown of Hamilton, Ohio.

Catching Up with...Gary Potempa

Gary Potempa knows what it's like to play on a Notre Dame football team that has a score to settle with the Southern California football team.

In October 1973 Potempa and his undefeated teammates hosted USC and running back Anthony Davis, who scored six touchdowns against the Irish in the Trojans' 45–23 victory the year before.

"The whole school was lit up," recalls Potempa, the team's starting middle linebacker. "There were pictures of Davis taped to the sidewalks all over campus, so students were walking on him all week."

Notre Dame put the clamps on Davis and defeated the Trojans 23–14 en route to the national championship. Potempa and a handful of his teammates earned a spot on the cover of that week's *Sports Illustrated*, along with Davis at the bottom of a pile of Irish defenders.

"I don't know if I've ever been so excited in my life," says Potempa of that game.

Potempa was just as accomplished off the field as he was on it, becoming one of three Irish—along with Bob Thomas and Dave Casper—to earn first-team academic All-America honors in 1973.

As Notre Dame's second-leading tackler in '73, Potempa was surprised and disappointed to be skipped in the NFL draft. But with the help of Irish assistant Tom Pagna and others, Potempa earned invites to a number of NFL and World Football League camps. After struggling for months with the decision, Potempa decided to enroll in dental school.

Despite an enjoyable and successful dental practice, Potempa admits, "Not a day goes by that I don't think about football."

The office is hardly an escape. It's common for patients to show up adorned with Notre Dame shirts and jerseys. Occasionally, a patient will show up in a Michigan shirt, calling into question the intelligence of anyone who would taunt a dentist before submitting to the drill.

Potempa has had the opportunity to coach his children in a wide variety of sports. Currently, Potempa helps coach at Carmel High School in Libertyville, Illinois, where his youngest child, Jimmy, was a senior running back and linebacker in 2006.

Potempa and his wife, Mary Pat, have four older children—Erin, a '99 Notre Dame grad who is an assistant prosecuting attorney in Lake County, Illinois; Dan, who has embarked on a football coaching career after playing at Iowa State and Milliken; and Sarah and Emily, who are living together and working in New York City.

Catching Up with...Wayne Bullock

Wayne Bullock claims that there is at least some question as to whether his two sons inherited their competitive nature from him. Bullock's two sons graduated from the University of North Carolina–Wilmington, where Patrick competed in the NCAA track-and-field championship as a high jumper before graduating and Brandon pursued his degree in clinical research.

"They're both competitive young men," says the proud father. "They want to compete with me at everything—you name it." But anybody who ever saw the former Notre Dame fullback play wouldn't entertain even a glimmer of doubt that Bullock's sons didn't come by their desire to compete naturally.

Bullock was a ferocious competitor, providing the perfect blend of toughness and speed for Ara Parseghian's teams of the early 1970s. As a junior Bullock led the '73 national champs with 752 yards rushing and 11 touchdowns. The following season, Bullock rushed for a team-high 855 yards and 12 touchdowns.

And Bullock was at his best when the stakes were highest. He was the game's leading rusher in Notre Dame's 24–23 victory over number one Alabama in the '73 Sugar Bowl and followed that up by earning the Orange Bowl offensive MVP award in Notre Dame's encore, a 13–11 victory over Alabama in Parseghian's last game as Irish head coach. Bullock relished the opportunity to play undefeated and top-ranked Alabama teams two years in a row.

"Everybody knew they were a good team and had great tradition, and we wanted to play them," Bullock recalls. "But when you go to Notre Dame, you know that you're going to get everybody's best shot because everybody wants to beat you more than anybody else on their schedule." The competition wasn't limited to Saturdays.

"There was a lot of talent at Notre Dame, and I feel that I was kind of fortunate to get to play," says Bullock modestly of his ability to earn a starting position over so many other high school greats. "And I always admired the guys on the prep team who came out every day and gave everything they had."

Bullock was a fifth-round draft pick of the NFL's San Francisco 49ers following his graduation, but a severe knee injury suffered as a rookie ended his playing career. After spending a few years back in his hometown of Newport News, Virginia, Bullock moved to North Carolina, where he still lives with his wife, Marcia.

A veteran of more than 25 years of human resources and labor relations management with MCI/WorldCom and its predecessors, Bullock also keeps busy golfing and with many church-related activities, along with closely following the fortunes of Notre Dame football.

"I bleed the Golden Dome," says Bullock. "I'm glad I made the decision to go there and I would love to get more involved.

"Charlie Weis is doing a great job," he offers. "They've definitely got the right man for the right job."

Yesterday's Heroes: Steve Niehaus

Steve Niehaus never was one to look deep into the future. Contingency plans rarely entered his mind and he left it to others to daydream about their ideal career or goals in life.

He was a simple young man perfectly suited for a position that—at its core—is founded in simplicity. A defensive lineman's role centers on plugging holes, making tackles, and pursuing the quarterback. The focus is on the here and now: the opposing jersey across the line of scrimmage that stands in the way of the most fundamental goals of defensive football.

"Pro football was not a lifelong goal of mine. I didn't look that far out and never had goals as a kid of being a doctor or a lawyer. I just wasn't like that," says Niehaus, whose roller-coaster career included consensus All-America honors at Notre Dame, the NFL Rookie of the Year trophy...and two major injuries in his college career, followed by another injury in pro ball that ultimately brought his playing days to a halt.

Niehaus, who became an area sales manager for Cincinnati-based Heidelberg Beverage Distribution, clearly had the attitude to excel in the role of defensive lineman. It was his unique combination of physical skills, which he humbly credits to "simple God-given talent," that placed him in elite status. Touted for his tremendous size and awesome strength, Niehaus played at another level due to his great speed, mobility, and relentless pursuit.

If you were the opponent and you were in the way, Niehaus was going to go through you or around you—either way, he was going to reach his target.

The 1972 college football season featured the return of freshman eligibility and Niehaus—who had started the opener versus Northwestern, two days shy of his 18th birthday—was slated to be featured on the cover of *Sports Illustrated*. But a midweek knee injury pushed his photo to one of the inside pages and, more importantly, ended his freshman season at the halfway point. One year later, he injured the other knee and missed the second half of that 1973 national championship season.

Some personnel limits in '74 forced Niehaus from his usual defensive tackle spot to defensive end, where he showcased his uncanny speed while chasing down world-class sprinters on end-around plays. He finally settled in back at tackle in 1975, becoming the first modern-era lineman to lead the Irish in tackles (113, in 10 games) en route to being a finalist for the Lombardi Award that is presented to the nation's top lineman.

The expansion Seattle Seahawks selected Niehaus with the second pick of the NFL draft, and he went on to be the league's Rookie of the Year for the 1976 season. A lingering arm injury ultimately derailed his three-year pro career (after a brief stint with the

Minnesota Vikings), and he later followed the lead of a friend into the beverage industry, starting as a Seattle-based sales representative for Pepsi.

"I was the 'big dog' coming out of high school and started four years at Notre Dame," he said. "Football had taken up all my time. I asked myself, 'What do I do now?' I had no career field picked out, no backup plan."

Nowadays—more than 30 years removed from his dominating senior season—Niehaus continues to keep his life simple, "staying low-key and out of the limelight." He has a grandson, Matt, to help occupy the free time and remains in contact with many of his former teammates, including fellow Cincinnati Moeller High School products Steve Sylvester and Andy Rohan.

He also has taken a quick liking to Irish head coach Charlie Weis, from one straight shooter to another.

"I didn't really know who Charlie Weis was, but I sure know who he is now. He has instilled a winning attitude, and that team won't accept defeat," says Niehaus.

"I live among so many Ohio State fans, and they have been giving us flack in recent years, but I took a lot of pride in watching that USC game in 2005. The Irish lost, but they gained so much from that game and it will show in the future," adds Niehaus, sounding more like a wily veteran with keen foresight and less like the live-for-the-present youngster.

"Any prospective player or student had to come away from that game with it making a great and positive impression on them," Niehaus said. "Charlie is pushing the right buttons to get us back on top, and that's something we all can be excited about."

Catching Up with…Robin Weber

Their national title hopes flickering in the closing minutes of the 1973 Sugar Bowl, Alabama head coach Bear Bryant and his players were worried about Notre Dame quarterback Tom Clements, bruising fullback Wayne Bullock, and All-American tight end Dave Casper.

Desperate to get the ball back for one last chance to over-come Notre Dame's 24–23 lead, Alabama had the Irish pinned, third-and-eight on the Notre Dame 2-yard line with a little over two minutes left in the game. The Tide never imagined that Weber, used extensively as a blocker in double tight end alignments, would do anything but block.

Notre Dame head coach Ara Parseghian called "Tackle Trap Pass Left," a play that the Irish had used to convert a two-point conversion earlier in the game. But that was with split end Pete Demmerle in the game, not Weber.

"I remember thinking to myself, 'Well, I can run a deep flag pattern—I did that in sandlot football,'" says a laughing Weber.

Weber's route was designed to free Casper open underneath. But Alabama blew the coverage, leaving Weber wide open. From the back of his end zone, Clements found Weber 37 yards down-field in front of the Alabama bench. The Irish had the first down, the victory, and Parseghian's second national championship.

Highly sought by every top program in the country, Weber committed to Notre Dame during his recruiting visit.

"They thought so much of me that they flew me up in February," he chuckles.

Parseghian, who was famous for not traveling to recruit, sealed the deal in his office. "I had [Texas head coach] Darrell Royal and [Arkansas head coach] Frank Broyles in my living room, but when Ara offered me that scholarship, I said, 'Okay.'

"I couldn't write a better script," he says. "It was exactly what I expected and quite a bit more."

After earning his degree from Notre Dame, Weber returned to his native Dallas, where he has owned a commercial real estate business. Along with his brother, Todd, and cousin Steve Vaughn, Weber acquired Whitestar Delivery, a third-party warehousing, transportation, and logistics company.

A week rarely passes without somebody reminding Weber of his Sugar Bowl catch, but Weber gives all the credit to his teammates.

"It was a night of big plays, and I just happened to be the last man through," he says. "You always remember the last man through.

"That's the way it has worked in my real estate career," explains Weber. "I'm real low-key, then...bang, I'll hit a big deal!"

Weber makes it back to Notre Dame frequently, including to serve as a coach during Notre Dame's fantasy football camp each summer. When asked to recount his famous play, Weber always credits his teammates, especially Casper, who jumped offside just before Weber's catch, prompting Parseghian to change from a run to a pass.

"I was in the right place at the right time," Weber laughs. "And I owe it all to Dave Casper."

chapter 6
The Dan Devine Years

Dan Devine coached the Fighting Irish to the 1977 national championship.

Dan Devine's 1977 national championship season included a pair of keynote victories—a midseason triumph over USC, in which the Irish debuted their green jerseys, and the Cotton Bowl win over top-ranked Texas, where the Notre Dame defense overwhelmed the Longhorns and Heisman winner Earl Campbell.

Catching Up with...Ken MacAfee

It might seem odd that the when the most decorated tight end in Notre Dame history looks back on his time at Notre Dame, his two fondest memories took place on the floor of the basketball arena.

As a 17-year-old high school football star, Ken MacAfee was recruited by hundreds of colleges. Irish head coach Ara Parseghian wasn't about to get into a bidding war.

"I told him that all these other schools were offering me cars and girlfriends," remembers MacAfee. "He laughed and said the only things he could offer me were a chance to play for a national championship and a chance to get the finest education in the country.

"That was all I wanted."

Four years later, MacAfee and his teammates were presented their 1977 national championship rings in a ceremony at the Athletic and Convocation Center. A few months after that, MacAfee was back in the ACC to receive his degree.

MacAfee was a three-time first-team All-American and the first lineman ever to win the Walter Camp Foundation Player of the Year award. He finished third in the 1977 Heisman Trophy voting after setting a Notre Dame record for tight ends with 54 catches.

"I never really entered college to achieve individual awards," MacAfee says. "I just wanted to be on a good team. People paid attention to me because we had a great team."

MacAfee was elected to the College Football Hall of Fame. He received the NCAA's Silver Anniversary Award for his postgraduate achievements.

As spectacular a football career as MacAfee had, he may have been more accomplished as a student. He earned his medical degree from the University of Pennsylvania while playing in the NFL.

After teaching for nearly a decade at Penn's school of dental medicine, MacAfee and his family returned to his native Massachusetts, where he has established a practice in oral and maxillofacial surgery.

MacAfee and his wife, Kathy, are the parents of a son, Dalton, and a daughter, Keely. Both children enjoy playing sports, but just as Parseghian did over 30 years ago, MacAfee makes sure academics come first.

Ken MacAfee, a three-time All-American, is still considered the greatest tight end to ever play for the Fighting Irish.

Catching Up with...Kris Haines

By his own admission, Kris Haines couldn't catch a cold during his freshman season as an Irish wide receiver. By the time he left Notre Dame, Haines had become famous for his exploits in the cold.

Haines was quarterback Joe Montana's favorite receiver in 1979, snagging 32 passes, including five touchdowns. Haines's greatest moment came during the 1979 Cotton Bowl in Dallas—"The Ice Bowl."

After trailing 34–12 with 7:26 to play, Notre Dame got the ball down 34–28 with 28 seconds to play and no timeouts remaining. With six seconds left, the Irish were on the Houston 8-yard line. After throwing incomplete for Haines, Montana came back with the same call. Haines made a diving catch, barely staying in bounds in the end zone.

The hands that had too often betrayed him during his freshman year were nearly frostbitten, but they were reliable. Irish head coach Dan Devine was so confident in Haines's hands that he ordered him to play without gloves in the brutal conditions.

"Dan Devine, bless his soul, came up to me before the game and said, 'James Lofton never wore gloves in Green Bay and he's in the Hall of Fame. You're not wearing gloves,'" recalls Haines with a laugh.

Haines is still enjoying the benefits of the remedy he employed at Notre Dame to improve his concentration and receiving—martial arts. He holds four different black belts and teaches martial arts to adults and children.

Haines, who makes his home in the Chicago area with his wife, Mary Ann, also teaches physical education while pursuing his master's degree at DePaul University. A veteran of several NFL seasons, Haines also works in football camps sponsored by the Chicago Bears and has been a frequent participant in the Blue-Gold flag football games and the Notre Dame football fantasy camps.

Catching Up with…Luther Bradley

Luther Bradley was an All-American defensive back at Notre Dame, a four-year starter, and a member of two national championship teams.

Thirty years later, Bradley has lost a little speed and a little quickness. However, he hasn't lost any of the bravado that all the great defensive backs need to have.

An enthusiastic fan of Irish head coach Charlie Weis's high-powered offense, Bradley laughs when asked what it would be like to play against Weis's attack.

"He always finds the weakness in a defense," Bradley notes. "They wouldn't be going after me."

Opposing defenses learned early not to go after Bradley. As a freshman, Bradley delivered a ferocious hit on USC's All-American wide receiver Lynn Swann.

On the Trojans' first offensive play, Pat Haden's pass to Swann and Bradley arrived simultaneously. Swann went flying, the ball went one way, and Swann's helmet went another. That play set the stage for Notre Dame's 23–14 victory, en route to the 1973 national championship.

A first-round pick in the 1978 NFL draft, Bradley played for the Detroit Lions for four seasons and has made Detroit his home ever since. Bradley and his wife, Sylvia, have four children—Rashida is a math teacher in New York City, Lutasha is a marketing representative in Los Angeles, Samuel graduated from North Carolina A&T, and Daniel attends Stanford University.

The diverse locations of their children give Luther and Sylvia plenty of chances to satisfy their travel bug when their busy schedules permit. Bradley is a longtime sales consultant with Blue Cross/Blue Shield while also serving as a trustee at their church and as chairman on the board of directors for the local chapter of Youth for Christ.

"We focus on disadvantaged children in the inner city," Bradley explains. "We're always trying to expose Christ and the Bible to people."

Bradley manages to find time to follow Notre Dame's football fortunes. As a member of the '77 team that donned green jerseys and thumped USC 49–19, Bradley gave a thumbs-up to the green jerseys worn by Notre Dame against USC in 2005 and against Army in '06.

"I was excited for them," he says. "The green jerseys are one of the treasures of Notre Dame."

Bradley is impressed with more than Weis's choice of uniform color.

"This guy is going to win a national championship," says Bradley. "He has got the goods."

Catching Up with...Ted Burgmeier

As a four-year monogram winner at Notre Dame, Ted Burgmeier learned how to battle.

Recruited by Ara Parseghian as an option quarterback, Burgmeier won playing time as a freshman by returning punts and playing in the defensive secondary. The following season, under new Irish head coach Dan Devine, Burgmeier earned the starting split end job. Against North Carolina, he turned a short pass from Joe Montana into a game-winning, 80-yard touchdown play in the closing minutes of a 21–14 comeback win.

During Burgmeier's senior season in 1977, "What tho' the odds" was more than a line from the "Victory March." As a starting corner-back, Burgmeier helped the underdog Irish rout Southern California 49–19. In that unforgettable green-jersey game, Burgmeier intercepted a pass to set up a touchdown, ran 21 yards on a fake field goal to lead to another touchdown, and passed to Tom Domin for a two-point conversion after a bobbled snap from center.

Ten weeks later, Notre Dame clinched the national championship by thrashing overwhelming favorite, undefeated, and top-ranked Texas 38–10 in the Cotton Bowl.

A fifth-round draft pick of the NFL Miami Dolphins, Burgmeier lasted until the final preseason roster cut before landing with the Kansas City Chiefs. After one season with the Chiefs, Burgmeier began to put his Notre Dame marketing degree to work. Little did he know, the real battles had yet to begin.

At age 27 Burgmeier was diagnosed with Hodgkin's disease. Following radiation treatment, Burgmeier was in remission until a recurrence in 1990. He underwent chemotherapy and has had a clean bill of health ever since. "I learned that cancer is not a death sentence," Burgmeier says. "I learned that I have a lot to live for, and I battled. I learned how to battle at Notre Dame."

At the top of Burgmeier's list of things to live for is his family. He married his high school sweetheart, Julie, while a student at Notre Dame. Three of the Burgmeier children are out of the household—son Chris and daughters Sarah and Stephanie are all married. Meanwhile, grade-school-age John has prompted Ted to get back into the coaching routine he knew while the older children were growing up.

Having coached his children in football, baseball, softball, and basketball, Burgmeier almost sounds as if he's having second thoughts, notwithstanding a very successful career in sales.

"Coaching is probably my true calling, although I never really gave it a chance," he reflects.

Burgmeier grew up in Dubuque, Iowa, and he returned to the area once his football career was over. "It's a great place to raise a family," he says. "And the kids love to come back—it's a real blessing."

Beyond lots of outdoor activities with the entire family, Burgmeier is active in the local Notre Dame alumni club and keeps in touch with many of his former teammates.

"We had great camaraderie on that team, and we still do."

The Comeback Kid: Joe Montana

Ask a football fan to name one player from Notre Dame—and the name Joe Montana probably remains the odds-on favorite to be the most common response.

Originally recruited by Ara Parseghian, Montana never actually played for him. Montana played on the Irish freshman squad as a rookie in 1974—while senior Tom Clements was starting at quarterback for the Notre Dame varsity in Parseghian's final season—then

Before he won four Super Bowls with the San Francisco 49ers, Joe Montana earned his "Comeback Kid" moniker at Notre Dame.

came off the bench on a handful of occasions as a sophomore in '75 to help the Irish win games under first-year coach Dan Devine. A national title in '77 helped cement Montana's place in the Irish history books. That, combined with his storied career as a four-time Super Bowl champion with the San Francisco 49ers, earned Montana his own permanent biography in the annual Notre Dame football media guide. Thanks in great part to his success in the pros, Montana's football years at both levels involved so many turns and details that chronicling his career was no small achievement.

For all the comebacks that marked his time with the Irish, none was more remarkable than the last in that series in what was Montana's final appearance as a collegian.

The scene was the Cotton Bowl in Dallas, where Notre Dame was playing for the second straight season and the fourth time in the 1970s. Both Notre Dame and Southwest Conference champion Houston came in with 8–3 overall records, so there was no particular championship on the line.

But thanks to a major ice storm the day before the game that cut attendance in half, January 1, 1979, was destined to go down as maybe the most remarkable of those Montana comebacks.

The Irish couldn't have struggled much more than they did in the opening half. Montana threw a pair of interceptions, the Irish lost a pair of fumbles, and the only reason the 20–12 intermission deficit wasn't worse was that the Cougars lost three fumbles of their own.

With Montana sitting in the locker room with hypothermia and slurping chicken broth in an attempt to warm up his system, things back on the frozen field went from bad to worse. None of the first four Irish third-period possessions produced a first down—and the third of those four ended in a blocked punt that Houston turned into a score and a 34–12 lead. When the Irish did get a first down with less than two minutes left in the third period, Montana—now back in the game—threw an interception two plays later.

Montana threw yet another interception and lost yet another fumble in the fourth quarter, but the Irish somehow mustered a comeback in the cold.

A blocked punt by the Irish and 33-yard return for a touchdown brought the score to 34–20 with 7:25 on the clock. Montana ran the final two yards of a 61-yard march to make it 34–28 after a two-point conversion at the 4:15 mark. Houston took a big gamble—and missed—on a fourth-and-one run attempt from its own 29, leaving Montana with 28 seconds. A Montana run for 11 yards and a pass to Kris Haines for 10 made it first down on the Cougars' 8 with six seconds left. Montana missed a throw to the corner of the end zone to Haines, then came back and completed the same play as time ran out. Joe Unis's PAT kick was nullified by a motion penalty—so the Dallas native did it again for the 35–34 final.

It may not have been the most amazing comeback in Notre Dame football history, but it was hard to imagine a more unlikely scenario for an Irish win, especially given the frozen field conditions.

"The guys on the team knew he wouldn't overheat," said Irish defensive back Dave Waymer of Montana's ability to deal with pressure situations.

"I'm convinced that's how Dracula sucks blood out of people's veins, that's what happened to Joe when he was born and the blood was replaced by ice water," said Devine later.

Said former Cincinnati Bengals receiver (now an NBC Sports commentator) Cris Collinsworth, whose Bengals lost to Montana's 49ers in Super Bowl XVI in Detroit, "Joe Montana is not human. I don't want to be blasphemous and call him God, but he's definitely somewhere in between."

Here are details of Montana's signature comebacks in his Notre Dame career:

Joe Montana's Comeback Statistics

Year	Opponent	Time Left	Deficit	Time On Field	Comp.	Att.	Yds.	TD	Final Score
1975	@North Carolina	5:11	14-6	1:02	3	4	129	2	21-14
1975	@Air Force	13:00	30-10	8:00	7	18	134	3	31-30
1977	@Purdue	11:00	24-14	6:00	9	14	154	2	31-24
1978	Pittsburgh	13:46	17-7	9:14	7	8	110	2	26-17
1978	@USC	12:59	26-6	10:00	11	15	201	2	25-27
1978	Houston (Dallas)	7:37	34-12	2:40	7	8	87	1	35-34
				36:56	44	67	815	12	

Note: Statistics are computed from time left until end of the game; in these six games combined, in 36:56 of clock time (about the same time an offense normally would be on the field in one full football game), Montana and his teammates put 114 points on the board.

Catching Up with...Jerome Heavens

Jerome Heavens took Notre Dame by storm and he's used a similar approach since he graduated Notre Dame more than 25 years ago.

As a freshman in 1975, Heavens rushed for 756 yards and 5.9 yards per carry to establish a Notre Dame freshman rushing

Jerome Heavens, shown here going over the top against USC in 1977, is the fifth-leading rusher in Notre Dame history.

record that stood until Darius Walker ran for 786 yards on 185 carries (4.2 yards per carry) in 2004. Still the fifth-leading career rusher in Notre Dame history, Heavens continues to hold Notre Dame's record for rushing yards in a single game by a freshman (148 yards in 18 carries against Georgia Tech).

After spending a couple of years pursuing a career in professional football, Heavens landed a sales position with Anheuser-Busch. Rather than work in his hometown market, home of Anheuser-Busch's corporate headquarters and where Budweiser is the undisputed king, the St. Louis native opted to work the Chicago market, where Anheuser-Busch was number four.

Anheuser-Busch is now a strong number two in Chicago, and Heavens jokes, "I've sold more Budweiser in Chicago than anyone but [late Chicago Cubs broadcaster] Harry Caray." While Heavens still may be chasing number one in Chicago, he and his team-mates reached the pinnacle in 1977, as Notre Dame won the national championship. During that season, Heavens became the first Notre Dame player ever to rush for 200 yards in a single game (200 yards against Army). He also fell just short of becoming the second player in Notre Dame history to rush for 1,000 yards in a single season (1994).

As a senior Heavens was elected a captain of the '78 squad, along with Joe Montana and Bob Golic. After an 0–2 start, the Irish rallied to win eight straight to win a berth in the Cotton Bowl, where Montana's heroics became the stuff of legend.

Despite all of the personal and team accomplishments Heavens experienced at Notre Dame, he looks back with the most pride at his degree in economics. After struggling in the classroom early in his career, Heavens graduated in three and a half years.

"I was the first in my family to graduate from a place like Notre Dame, and it was great to see how my family looked up to that," he says, giving special credit to his mother for influencing his deci-sion to attend Notre Dame.

"I wish I could turn back the hands of time and do it all over again," Heavens says.

Thanks to his 101-yard performance on 22 carries, Heavens helped Notre Dame defeat top-ranked Texas 38–10 in the 1978 Cotton Bowl en route to its 1977 national championship.

Heavens remains close to his family. In addition to his wife, Patti, he spends lots of time with his grown sons and with his parents and two siblings in the St. Louis area.

He also remains very passionate about Notre Dame, being involved in the Notre Dame Club of Chicago and never missing a game on television. "I'm the biggest fan for Notre Dame—and not only the athletes," he says. "I tried my best to be a part of a great institution, and I feel extremely honored to have been a part of Notre Dame."

Catching Up with…Chuck Male

He could have been "Rudy."

A lifelong Fighting Irish fan, he was initially denied admission to Notre Dame. Undaunted, he gained admission as a transfer student, but that wasn't enough. He had to make the football team. Once he did that, Irish placekicker Chuck Male even outdid the most famous walk-on in Notre Dame history by etching his name in the Notre Dame record book.

The highlight of Male's career came in the first game of the 1979 season when he accounted for all of Notre Dame's scoring in a 12–10 upset of number six Michigan in Ann Arbor. And while Hollywood hasn't come calling, Male's heroics were captured by an ABC-TV national telecast.

A native of Kansas City, Missouri, who moved with his family to Mishawaka when he was in sixth grade, Male enrolled at Western Michigan University. He earned the Broncos' starting place-kicker's spot before gaining admission to Notre Dame during his freshman year in Kalamazoo. Faced with the decision of whether to give up his hard-won position at Western Michigan for an uncertain journey at Notre Dame, Male followed his dreams and enrolled at Notre Dame.

Much like the character in the movie, Male's battle was far from over. It was hardly a given that he would make the team, let alone play in a game.

"I was kicking by myself on Cartier Field before spring practice started when [Irish head coach] Dan Devine was running on the track," Male recalls. "He stopped running and came over to me and said, 'Go inside and tell [assistant coach] Hank Kuhlman that you're on the team and you need equipment.'

"Later, Coach Devine would tell people that he 'discovered' me—I felt like I was a continent or something," laughs Male. It was a "discovery" that paid big dividends for Devine and the Irish. Male won the starting kicking job in '78 following the graduation of four-year starter Dave Reeve. Male's 13 field goals as a senior in '79 tied Reeve for the Notre Dame single-season record, and Male still stands 10th on Notre Dame's all-time list.

After a couple of near misses attempting to earn spots with the Chicago Bears and Denver Broncos, Male began working as a commercial real estate broker with CB Richard Ellis in Cincinnati. He's been there ever since, as he raises three children with his wife, Sossie.

Eldest son Charlie was a senior starting wide receiver in 2006 on the nationally ranked St. Xavier High School football team, while younger brother Sam quarterbacked the junior varsity team as a sophomore and is a standout baseball player. Younger sister Josie was a freshman in '06 at Ursuline Academy, where she runs cross country.

And just as his father once did for him, Male is instilling in his children a love for Notre Dame. As youngsters, they watched Notre Dame's student managers paint the football helmets and even helped get the players' lockers ready for the game.

The next generation—it almost sounds like the script to a movie.

Catching Up with...John Scully

John Scully hates to be labeled—and he lives like it. Scully became an All-American center for Notre Dame in 1980 after switching from offensive tackle. In the NFL, Scully moved to guard, where he was a perennial starter for the Atlanta Falcons.

Since retiring from football, Scully has continued to defy labeling. A lifelong musician who almost chose to play football at Penn State, motivated largely by that university's school of music, Scully embarked on a career writing and producing commercial music—from CDs to television and radio commercials. He gained perhaps his greatest notoriety for writing and recording "Here Come the Irish," a song about the University of Notre Dame that—wouldn't you know it—doesn't contain a single explicit reference to football.

The song illustrates Scully's willingness to take on a daunting challenge. It wasn't as if Scully and coproducer Jim Tullio had never heard the Notre Dame "Victory March."

"We wanted a distinctive effort," Scully says. "But we wanted something perpendicular, not opposite."

The universal acclaim that greeted the release of "Here Come the Irish" left no doubt that Scully and Tullio had hit their target.

"The lyrics are from an observer's point of view," Scully explains. "It doesn't matter if you're an All-American, the president of the university, or a freshman in his first semester, everyone ends up being a brick in the wall."

Scully is proud of what he and his teammates accomplished at Notre Dame. The 1980 team he captained as a senior surprised nearly everybody by climbing to the top of the polls by November. But Scully doesn't spend much time reliving those days.

"We get to go out every day and write our own biographies," he says. "What I did at Notre Dame is ancient history."

Two labels that Scully does gladly embrace are those of husband and father. Living in Joliet, Illinois, with his wife and two daughters—Britt enrolled as a freshman at Notre Dame in the fall of '06—Scully has changed labels once again, entering the commercial insurance field.

The early indications are that Scully will be labeled a success once again.

Catching Up with...Tom Gibbons

On the crowded and impressive résumé of Tom Gibbons, Notre Dame and Indiana seem little more than small blips on the radar screen.

Currently the president of Sargent, an aerospace subsidiary of Dover Corporation, Gibbons grew up in Alexandria, Virginia, and has lived all over the country.

But as they say, home is where the heart is.

Notre Dame is where Gibbons battled his way to the top of the Notre Dame depth chart to become a three-year starter at defensive back and senior captain for Dan Devine's last Irish team.

It's where he hit the books as hard as he hit opposing receivers, earning academic All-America honors en route to a degree in aerospace engineering. It's where Gibbons got to know his future bride, Lexi (although the two actually met for the first time at a party for incoming Notre Dame and Saint Mary's freshmen from the Alexandria area).

Notre Dame is even beginning to feel like home to the Gibbons's five children. Tom's father graduated from the Naval Academy (as did Tom's eldest son, T.J.), but switched his cheering allegiances to Notre Dame during his son's four years on the Irish squad.

"Blood is pretty thick," Tom offers.

Tom and Lexi nearly got a chance to figure out exactly how thick, but injuries brought T.J.'s football career to a premature end before he claimed a spot on Navy's varsity.

"I almost had to cheer for Navy," Gibbons confesses.

The other Gibbons children also are following paths not unfamiliar to their parents. Daniel is studying engineering at Virginia Tech, while Sean played cornerback for Salpointe Catholic High School in Tucson, Arizona.

"He got his mother's speed," says his father.

Keegan is also playing high school football, as a middle linebacker and fullback. "He's got a hard head," says Gibbons, without elaborating on the genetics.

As the only daughter, Meaghan unquestionably takes after her mother.

"She definitely rules the roost," laughs Tom. Unlike her older brothers, Meaghan has yet to attend a football game at Notre Dame, but that will change.

Despite Tom's career, Lexi's booming real estate business, and all of the children's sports and other activities, the Gibbons family still travels back to Notre Dame at least once a year.

"It's home," Tom says.

Catching Up with...Jim Stone

Rarely has a player demonstrated greater perseverance at Notre Dame than Jim Stone.

A highly regarded running back who played baseball with future PGA star Fred Couples at Kennedy High School in Seattle,

Stone displayed his considerable talent from the moment he arrived at Notre Dame, earning a monogram as a freshman on Notre Dame's 1977 national championship team.

But playing time was hard to come by, with Notre Dame's impressive stable of veteran running backs, including Vagas Ferguson, who graduated just one year ahead of Stone as Notre Dame's all-time leading rusher, and Jerome Heavens.

Despite an MVP performance in the 1980 Blue-Gold game, Stone started his senior season as the number two tailback behind sophomore Phil Carter, who Stone helped recruit to Notre Dame from Tacoma, Washington.

But when Carter was injured on the final carry of a 254-yard performance against Michigan State (one shy of Ferguson's all-time Notre Dame record at the time), Stone finally got his chance to start. All he did was run for 224 yards against Miami's top-10 rushing defense.

"There was no doubt in my mind I would be ready, but I would be lying if I told you that I said I knew I'd get over 200 yards in my first start," Stone admits.

His performance against Miami was hardly a fluke. He ran for over 100 yards in each of Notre Dame's next two games—including a 122-yard performance against Army—before topping the 200-yard mark again in his fourth start, with 211 yards against Navy.

Stone both sparked and epitomized the 1980 Notre Dame squad, as head coach Dan Devine's final Irish squad surprised all of the experts by winning its first seven games en route to the number one ranking in early November. Stone, who had led Notre Dame in kickoff returns as a sophomore and a junior, once again topped the Irish in that department, while also leading the '80 team with 908 rushing yards.

After a brief stint in the NFL, Stone starred for two seasons with the Chicago Blitz of the United States Football League before moving back to South Bend with his wife, former Notre Dame cheerleader Phyllis Washington.

Jim Stone earned his first career start during his senior season against Miami on October 11, 1980, and responded with a 224-yard effort on 38 carries in leading the Irish to a 32–14 victory. He went on to rush for 100-plus yards in three consecutive outings following that game, including a 211-yard performance in the Irish's 33–0 victory over Navy on November 1. He finished the season as the team's leading rusher with 908 yards on 192 carries.

The couple now lives in New Jersey, where Jim is a sales executive with Merial, the world's largest animal health care enterprise, and Phyllis is senior director of marketing for Merck & Co., Inc., and also serves on Notre Dame's board of trustees.

Their son, Alex, entertained offers to play football and basketball at several Ivy League schools and received an invitation to walk on to Notre Dame's football team. Alex chose to attend New Jersey Institute of Technology, where he is pursuing a degree in business and communications and playing a key role on the basketball team as it transitions from NCAA Division II to Division I.

In his extensive public speaking, Stone talks about his time at Notre Dame. "It's such a unique experience, that sometimes you can't understand it while you're there," he says. "But I always tell people to be patient, and when it's your turn, take advantage of it."

chapter 7
The Gerry Faust Years

While nobody doubted Gerry Faust's passion, he struggled—by Fighting Irish standards—to a 30–25–1 record during his career at Notre Dame. Photo courtesy of AP/Wide World Photos.

Faust's 1984 Irish team confounded the experts when, after three straight losses at home, Notre Dame traveled to Baton Rouge to face the sixth-ranked Tigers and knocked them off 30–22. That win put Faust on the cover of *Sports Illustrated* in the following issue under the headline "I'm Gonna Make It!"

Harry Oliver: The Unlikely Hero

Maybe few Notre Dame football players ever qualified as a more unlikely hero than Harry Oliver did on September 20, 1980.

A junior place-kicker from Cincinnati, Ohio, Oliver, a left-footed, soccer-style kicker, had been known mostly as a Moeller High School sidekick of Irish teammates and high school classmates Tim Koegel, Bob Crable, and Dave Condeni.

As a sophomore the previous season, Oliver's contributions had included only field goals of 27 and 38 yards in a junior varsity game against Wisconsin.

He had come into the '80 season as Notre Dame's number one kicker, yet his only varsity attempt to that point came on a successful 36-yard field goal in the 1980 season-opening win against Purdue.

That brings us to Michigan's visit to Notre Dame Stadium two weeks later.

In a back-and-forth event that already had seen the lead change four times, Michigan gained what appeared to be a clinching advantage with a 78-yard, 10-play drive that culminated in a Wolverine touchdown pass—to a player, Craig Dunaway, who had never before caught a pass—with 41 seconds remaining. That gave Michigan a 27–26 advantage after a missed two-point conversion pass. That drive came after senior quarterback Mike Courey had led the Irish 74 yards on 11 plays for a 26–21 Notre Dame lead at the 3:03 mark of the final period.

After Michigan took the lead, Irish coach Dan Devine put the game in the hands of heralded but untested freshman quarterback Blair Kiel, who had yet to throw a pass in a college game. Here's the sequence from there, with Kiel throwing four straight times out of a shotgun formation:

- On first down from the Irish 20, Michigan was called for interference on a jump-ball-type throw to Tony Hunter right in front of the Michigan bench. That turned into a 32-yard penalty gain and gave Notre Dame another first down on the Michigan 48 with 31 seconds left. "It was a

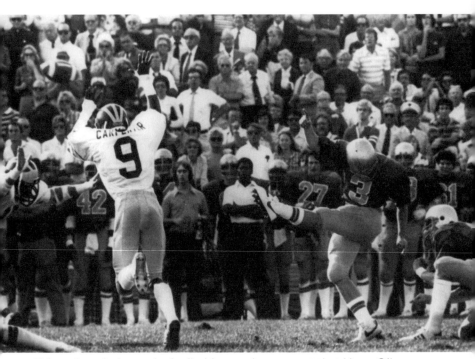

When the wind seemingly died just at the moment that Harry Oliver attempted his 51-yard field goal to beat Michigan in 1980, he instantly became a part of Irish lore.

bad pass. Came down like a dying punt. We were lucky it wasn't intercepted," said Kiel.

- A pass to Pete Holohan went incomplete, as did one to Dean Masztak. On third-and-10, Kiel found Phil Carter over the middle for nine yards, with now 11 seconds left. "It wasn't a good start. The first two were almost intercepted," said Kiel.
- On fourth-and-one from the Michigan 39, Kiel hit Hunter on the Irish sideline for five yards, leaving Notre Dame on the Michigan 34 with four seconds remaining.

That brought in Oliver to attempt a 51-yard field goal.

Differing reports suggested anywhere from a 15- to 20-mph wind in Oliver's face. The breeze had been strong enough that Kiel earlier had been able to launch a 69-yard punt, followed by a

59-yard quick kick on the next possession, that proved to be the longest of his career.

But, somehow, the wind apparently stopped just as Oliver was attempting the 51-yard kick, at least that's what Tim Koegel (the holder on the play) claims. And that may have made all the difference. Oliver's attempt barely skipped across the goal post as time expired for the 29–27 Irish win—despite only 234 total yards by the Irish—over the number 14 Wolverines.

Notre Dame survived despite the fact its first four possessions of the second half accounted for 11 plays from scrimmage for a net of minus-six yards.

"You know, just as I placed the ball down, the wind died down. Almost stopped. I knew then we'd make it," said Koegel.

"This was the all-time, all-time, all-time moment," said Devine. "I've never seen Harry kick one that far, but it went through today and that's all I care about. He's a heck of a nice kid. He was a nice kid even before he kicked it."

"I didn't look up until I heard everyone screaming and I knew Harry had made it," said Crable.

It was ever so unlikely for Oliver, who had put his team in a potential bind by missing a third-period extra point.

"I couldn't look. I looked away," said Carter.

The dramatic ending produced one of the more memorable postgame scenes as students and fans rushed the field. The Mutual Radio call by Tony Roberts, then in his first year as voice of the Irish, became well-known to Irish fanatics for its own dramatic effect.

The moment was preserved in a classic black-and-white photograph showing Oliver's follow-through and the ball eluding the outstretched hands of two Michigan defenders. In the background of the shot can be seen Notre Dame president Rev. Theodore M. Hesburgh, C.S.C., and university executive vice president Rev. Edmund P. Joyce, C.S.C., watching from the stands.

The photo was taken by Peter Romzick, a student who was shooting for The Dome, Notre Dame's yearbook.

Among the defensive line starters that afternoon for Michigan was senior Mike Trgovac, who made eight tackles in the game and later became an Irish assistant coach from 1992 to 1994.

Catching Up with...Phil Carter

Even today, catching up with Phil Carter is no easy feat.

It's not that Carter is evasive—he's more than happy to take time out of a hectic schedule to talk.

As a proud husband and father, Carter speaks glowingly of his wife, Linda, daughter, Kennedy, and son, Garret. Carter's joy is obvious when he shares stories of young people whose lives have been transformed thanks to the YMCAs where he has worked. In relating the turnaround he led at the YMCA in Kalamazoo, Michigan, Carter first mentions the assistance provided by former Irish teammates.

It quickly becomes apparent that catching up with Carter means getting a peek at a man who is not at the center of his own universe.

Even as the star tailback on Notre Dame's 1980 football team that reached number one in the polls eight weeks into that season, Carter didn't buy the hype.

When pressed to reflect on his playing days, Carter recalls the struggles as well as the glory. Even when talking about his 200-yard performance against Michigan State in 1980, Carter speaks of fumbling on his 40th and final carry—losing three yards and the school's single-game rushing record.

"I've been gifted with a little athletic ability," he allows, "but I was never the best athlete on the team."

Coming from a player who completed his Notre Dame career behind only Vagas Ferguson and George Gipp on the school's all-time career rushing list, Carter's claim may smack of false modesty. The life Carter has led since graduation says otherwise.

While former teammates with less impressive Notre Dame résumés enjoyed success in the NFL, Carter quickly went from volunteer instructor at a YMCA in his hometown of Tacoma, Washington, to full-time employee. Before long, Carter was executive director, responsible for everything from fund-raising to pitching in when necessary to make the place look good.

"Whatever it takes," Carter says simply.

Carter does whatever it takes because he cares.

"My biggest passion is to give everybody an opportunity to succeed," he says. "There has always been this thing of excuses.

"I can be a resource. I want those things for everyone—to graduate high school, to go to college, to get a good job. It's going to be hard, young people have to believe they can do whatever it takes to get there. That's why I'm here—to be a solution."

Just like he was when the game was on the line for Notre Dame.

Catching Up with...Tom Thayer

Whether you spot Tom Thayer in the crowded confines of a radio broadcast booth high above Soldier Field or surfing the endless expanse of the brilliant blue Pacific Ocean off the coast of Hawaii, you can be sure of one thing—Thayer has put in hours of time preparing to engage in his passion.

An honorable mention All-American offensive lineman for Notre Dame in the early 1980s, Thayer finished his 10th season in 2006 as an analyst for Chicago Bears radio broadcasts. Thayer, who grew up a Bears fan in Joliet, Illinois, and started on the only Bears team to win the Super Bowl, treats the role as a full-time job.

To prepare, Thayer attends every Bears training camp session and nearly every practice during the season, and watches dozens of hours of video.

"It's too easy to say something's bad or something's good—it's usually not that simple," Thayer explains. "You want to have respect for the players and be specific when you're describing a player's performance. The players know that when I say something, it comes from having watched hours and hours of tape."

Once the season is over, Thayer leaves for his second home in Hawaii. But Thayer's days aren't an endless succession of mai tais and suntan oil—he's up daily before dawn in search of giant waves.

"Surfing is a very individualistic sport; if you're serious about it, you can't wait around until a bunch of your friends get interested in it," Thayer explains. "But when you pull up to the ocean and see the surf and that there are big waves that are going to challenge you, it's the same feeling in the pit of your stomach as when you're driving to the stadium to play a football game on a Sunday morning.

"It keeps my blood flowing."

There is one thing more important to Thayer than football and surfing—his family. Thayer is the youngest of five siblings, and his parents welcomed three more children into the household after neighboring parents died in a plane crash.

"My parents have been married more than 50 years, and the reason we all respect each other so much and care about each other so much is the commitment that my parents had to all of us," says Thayer.

For now, Thayer is content to play the roles of devoted son and uncle to a swarm of nieces and nephews. Given Thayer's passion for family and watching football tape, don't be surprised if his future holds parenthood and coaching.

There may just be more to catch up with Tom Thayer about in the future.

Catching Up with...Tim Scannell

Tim Scannell enjoyed more than his share of success as a Notre Dame football player. So when he heard a person in Notre Dame Stadium calling his name during a game, Scannell figured it was an autograph request.

Once the fan had Scannell's attention, he made his plea: "Hey, do you think you could get Allen Pinkett to sign this jersey for me?" the fan pleaded, angling for the signature of Pinkett, one of Notre Dame's all-time leading rushers.

Scannell, an Irish captain and second-team All-American as a senior offensive guard, laughs as he recounts the story.

"You need to know your role in life," he says.

After spending time in the Dallas Cowboys camp as an undrafted free agent, Scannell had a stint as a graduate assistant coach on Lou Holtz's Notre Dame coaching staff during the 1987–1988 season.

During those two years, Scannell earned a Notre Dame MBA and also learned a number of lessons outside the classroom. He applied those lessons first as a United States Secret Service agent and then in a steady rise through the corporate world, culminating in his current position as president of Stryker Spine, a division of the health-care giant Stryker Corporation.

"Simply watching Lou Holtz lead and drive the organization on to greatness taught me lessons and gave me examples that I can emulate to this day," Scannell offers.

Greatness—at least as measured in wins and losses—was more elusive during Scannell's Notre Dame playing days under head coach Gerry Faust, but Scannell sees a great link between his experiences as a player and his success in the world beyond Notre Dame.

"Intensity and competitive spirit were baked into you," says Scannell. "The pressure of competing against very formidable opponents, overcoming adversity, and surviving to fight another day are lessons that have served me well in my career."

At one point in his career, Scannell was entrusted with protecting the president of the United States and his family. Today, Scannell's first family consists of his wife, Brigid, and their three children, Shane, Spencer, and Kenna.

The Scannells return to Notre Dame often, where visits to the Grotto, Sacred Heart Basilica, and other campus sites "energize and humble" the former star.

"In the grand scheme of life," Scannell said, "Notre Dame always helps remind you of what's really important."

chapter 8
The Lou Holtz Years

Lou Holtz, who arrived in South Bend in 1986, is credited with returning Notre Dame to its rightful spot among the nation's elite programs.

Lou Holtz was happy to utilize anything to motivate his team—and a Friday's waiter helped him immensely prior to Notre Dame's 1992 Sugar Bowl match with third-ranked Florida. The waiter told Holtz this joke— "What's the difference between Notre Dame and Cheerios? Cheerios belong in a bowl"— and Holtz made great use of that line prior to his team's 39–28 upset win.

Tim Brown: Victorious Amid Defeat

Seldom in nearly 25 years of football was Tim Brown part of a winning organization. Yet, in an ironic twist of fate, that's how he became such a winner on and off the field.

It goes back to his days as a varsity member of Woodrow Wilson High in Dallas, Texas, from 1981 to 1983. During Brown's career, Wilson was 4–25–1, winning one game in his sophomore campaign, two as a junior, and one as a senior.

"The lack of success by our high school team helped me in a way because it made me play harder than ever each week," said Brown during his student days at Notre Dame. "I figured that if I wanted to get a college scholarship, I would have to make each play count and take nothing for granted.

"Every time I touched the ball, I said to myself I'd better do something good with it or I'd never make it anywhere."

Although overlooked by many high school blue-chip publications, the diamond in the rough received enough notice to take official visits as a senior to Notre Dame, Iowa, SMU, Oklahoma, and Nebraska. The decision came down to SMU—located only two miles from his home—or Gerry Faust's Irish. Confronted with immense pressure to stay in state with a program that was handed the NCAA death penalty in the late 1980s, Brown, with some inspiration from his family, opted for the Fighting Irish.

Four years later, after accepting the Heisman Trophy as the nation's premier college player, Brown was asked whether Notre Dame's name was what helped him receive the award.

"I'm not going to apologize for going to Notre Dame," Brown replied. "I did it to better myself as a person."

That mission was fulfilled—and then some—as an athlete, a current entrepreneur, NFL analyst, husband, and father.

In 1995 Brown became the national chairman of Athletes & Entertainers for Kids and 9-1-1 for Kids, and his service to others has earned him just as much respect as his nine Pro Bowl appearances with the Los Angeles/Oakland Raiders.

"I was fortunate to grow up in a wonderful, supportive, and loving family," Brown said. "I realized early on that many children are not as fortunate and just finding a meal is a daily fight for thousands of youth." Often characterized as the "anti-Raider" for his clean-cut background, Brown still was confident and brash enough to clash with mercurial Raiders owner Al Davis, or even tell a deeply religious teammate that it was fine to read the Bible, but he better start reading the playbook, too.

As a Notre Dame freshman, Brown was the first player to handle the ball to open the 1984 campaign against Purdue. The play resulted in a fumbled kickoff return that the Boilermakers recovered and turned into a score in their 23–21 upset victory.

How's that for a grand entry?

Several weeks later the Irish lost their third straight at home (for the first time since 1956) and were booed as they walked off their home turf with a 3–4 record.

"Most guys here came from state champion teams and were always used to winning. They were really down, but I'd think, 'Oh man, what's wrong? We've already won three games,'" said Brown laughing.

In his four seasons, the Irish were only 25–21, including 0–2 in two bowl appearances. He was part of the lone back-to-back losing seasons at the school in 1985 with Faust (5–6) and 1986 with Lou Holtz (5–6). When Holtz arrived, the new Irish head coach vowed "the only way we're going to keep the ball out of Tim Brown's hands is if they intercept the snap from center."

Utilizing Brown in the backfield, at wideout and as both a kick and punt returner, Holtz maximized Brown's skills and saw him produce, to this day, the two most all-purpose yards gained in a season at Notre Dame—first with 1,937 (1986) and then 1,847 (1987).

Brown made Fighting Irish football hip again, and his brilliance in the 1986–1987 season helped attract premier recruits such as Raghib "Rocket" Ismail, Ricky Watters, Todd Lyght, Chris Zorich, and a plethora of others, into the fold during Holtz's halcyon years from 1988 to 1993, when the Irish were 64–9–1, with one national title and two debatable number two finishes.

Brown's senior year did see the Irish produce their best record (8–4) in seven years, but even then, they closed with consecutive

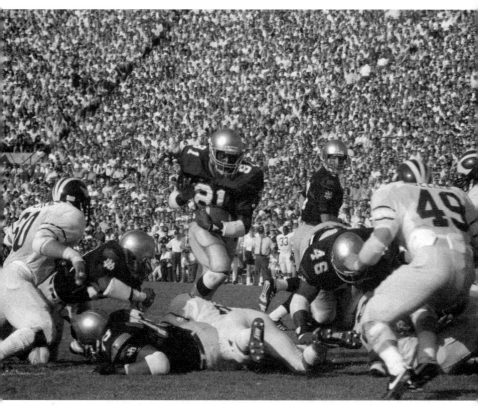

Tim Brown was the most electric offensive weapon Notre Dame has ever had, both as a kick returner and as a receiver.

losses to Penn State (21–20), national champ Miami (24–0), and Texas A&M in the Cotton Bowl (35–10).

Even in the NFL, the sixth pick of the 1988 draft experienced only six playoff wins. From 1991 through 2000, the once-proud Raiders organization had only one playoff victory and didn't even advance to postseason action in seven of those 10 seasons. Brown's best individual campaign came in 1997 (104 catches, 1,408 yards)—a year the Raiders finished 4–12 before hiring a new coach, Jon Gruden.

The football timing never seemed to be quite right for Brown. The year after he graduated from Notre Dame, the Irish won the national title. The year after Gruden departed Oakland, he led

Tampa Bay to the Super Bowl title with a 48–21 victory versus Brown's Raiders.

Yet, when Brown joined Gruden at Tampa Bay in 2004 for his final NFL season, the Bucs finished 5–11, slightly better than the 4–12 mark of Brown's final Raiders team the previous season.

The timing and circumstances weren't quite right for Brown to join Charlie Weis's coaching staff in the winter of 2005, either, but the Notre Dame icon still has his heart with the Irish, just as he did more than two decades earlier. So when Weis called Brown to serve as an honorary coach at the 2005 Blue-Gold game with Joe Montana, Joe Theismann, and Zorich, Brown responded enthusiastically. "This was probably one of the biggest thrills I've had in a long time," said Brown of the 2005 spring game played in frigid conditions. "It almost makes me think about coaching. Being on the sidelines and having young kids come up to you and say, 'Teach me your stance'—it was a blast for me."

Now he knows how others felt watching him play—win or lose. Amidst so many football defeats, Brown never lost his perspective.

Catching Up with...Darrell "Flash" Gordon

In a "Flash," his playing days at Notre Dame were over.

Fifty-four months and five football seasons following that initial 700-mile trek from his home in New Jersey to his dorm room in Alumni Hall, Darrell Gordon stood on the turf of Sun Devil Stadium a national champion. Gordon earned the last of 16 career starts at the 1989 Fiesta Bowl in his final collegiate game played.

The sun set gloriously across the desert sky that memorable January 2, but the sun was just beginning to rise on Gordon's lifetime of service to others. And despite all his travels and accomplishments, those Gordon would help most were children who often never left the four blocks surrounding their own homes.

His purpose? The education and development of youth, especially those in need.

His method? R-I-C-H-E-R, a moniker developed during his work with the NCAA but inspired by his days at Notre Dame, based on (R) Respect, (I) Integrity, (C) Caring, (H) Harmony, (E) Excellence, and (R) Responsibility.

"Those were the great principles that I began to develop at Notre Dame," says Gordon. "My time there introduced me to the diversity that I needed to succeed in life. Notre Dame opened my eyes to opportunities that I never saw before. It was a fabulous experience in learning how to be a better leader."

Gordon earned his bachelor's degree in economics and business in 1988, a master's degree in science and administration in 1989, and his J.D. from Northern Kentucky's Chase College of Law in 1997. In between, Gordon's journey would take him from an internship on Wall Street at the New York Stock Exchange to a program of study in nonprofit management at the Harvard Business School; from managerial positions with Advance Drainage Systems in southern Ohio to a professorship in sports law at Ball State University in central Indiana; from a clerkship with a prominent Cincinnati law firm to a position with the sports management firm IMG; and from Kansas City to Indianapolis and a career with the NCAA, where Gordon worked in the Membership Service Group and also coordinated the "Stay in Bounds" program that promotes sportsmanship among youth.

Gordon's vocation, however, would ultimately lead him to the Wernle Children's Home, a residential treatment behavioral healthcare agency in Richmond, Indiana, whose primary goal is the rehabilitation of children afflicted by such problems as abuse, neglect, mental illness, or conduct disorder. As Wernle's chief executive officer since 2001, Gordon oversees all aspects of the organization, including finance, development, philanthropy, and control.

"To finally see those youth have hope is what I strive for," says Gordon. "There is a life that they have not considered before coming to us. The program is in place to allow youth to have faith and confidence and be able to take care of themselves independently of their families. My passion is to put all of those pieces together to let the kids have an opportunity to get better."

For his efforts, Gordon has been honored by both his alma maters, receiving the William D. Reynolds Award from Notre Dame in recognition of his work for the betterment of the quality of life for youth, as well as the Exceptional Service Award honoring those graduates of the Chase College of Law who exhibit the ideals of the law school through daily contributions of service.

Gordon was known as "Flash" on the gridiron. His impact away from it, however, will last much longer than any moment in time.

Catching Up with...Reggie Ho

He was the most unlikely of heroes.

Few Notre Dame fans had even heard of Reggie Ho prior to September 10, 1988. But with three field goals that night, the 5'5", 135-pound walk-on kicker had done more than his share to help the young Irish in their bid to knock off ninth-ranked Michigan.

But even more would be required of Ho, playing in his first-ever Notre Dame game. Michigan's Mike Gillette booted a 49-yard field goal with 5:39 remaining in the fourth quarter, giving the Wolverines a 17–16 lead over the 13th-ranked Irish.

Notre Dame drove to the Michigan 9-yard line, where on fourth down and with 1:13 to play in the game, Ho converted his fourth field goal of the night, a 26-yarder.

The season-opening upset started Notre Dame on its way to a 12–0 season and the national championship, capped by a 34–21 win over West Virginia in the Fiesta Bowl.

"Standing on the sideline of the Fiesta Bowl with the clock winding down, it kind of dawned on me that we were going to win a national championship," recalls Ho. "It was great to bring back some glory to Notre Dame."

Today, Ho lives in the Philadelphia area with his wife, Maromi, and son, Ethan. A cardiologist at the Thomas Jefferson University Hospital, Ho's subspecialty is electrophysiology.

Patients often recognize Ho for his football exploits at Notre Dame. It's a good bet those patients are reassured by knowing that Ho has been coming through under pressure for many years.

Catching Up with...The Three Amigos: Legendary Linebackers Wes Pritchett, Michael Stonebreaker, and Frank Stams

As the "Three Amigos," Frank Stams, Michael Stonebreaker, and Wes Pritchett terrorized teammates, their coaches, and opposing offenses while leading Notre Dame to the 1988 national championship. Years later, opponents and coaches are finally safe, but the trio still terrorizes each other at every opportunity.

"Frank, when did you get out of jail?" bellows Pritchett into the telephone as he greets Stams.

"I've got one of those bracelets," responds Stams, without missing a beat.

"You can saw through those things, you know," offers Pritchett.

"I know, but I'm afraid that they'll put a chip in me next if I do that," explains Stams.

Stonebreaker, the youngest of the group, explains his decision to attend Notre Dame.

"Wesley Pritchett was my host on my recruiting visit to Notre Dame. After spending a weekend with Wes, there was nowhere else in the world I wanted to be," says Stonebreaker, the sarcasm dripping from his voice.

Believe it or not, the Three Amigos hit opponents even harder.

Whether it was Pritchett sending West Virginia All-American quarterback Major Harris to the sideline early with a devastating hit in the Fiesta Bowl or Stams burying USC's Rodney Peete into the turf while Stan Smagala returned one of Peete's errant passes for a touchdown, the trio set the tone for Notre Dame's 12–0 season.

To hear the Amigos tell it, their ability to wreak havoc on the football field was due at least in part to their ability to wreak havoc off the field.

"The person who was the glue, the person who really put it all together, was Barry Alvarez," says Stams of the '88 Irish defensive coordinator, later the very successful head coach (and now athletics director) at Wisconsin.

The 1998 national championship linebacking squad of Wes Pritchett (top), Frank Stams (center), and Michael Stonebreaker (bottom)—also known as the Three Amigos—wreaked havoc on opposing teams.

"Our personalities fit very well with Barry's," elaborates Pritchett. "He believed that you had to keep the guys loose."

Of course, Notre Dame head coach Lou Holtz wasn't exactly known for promoting "looseness."

"Lou was a master at keeping you on your toes," says Stams, "and he had a great complement in Barry."

"Barry let us be ourselves," says Pritchett.

"Our biggest motivation was to keep Coach Holtz away from us in practice," says Stams.

"If we didn't play well, Coach Holtz would be over on the defensive side of the ball," explains Stonebreaker.

Presumably, Holtz was working with the offense in practice the day Stams noticed something out of the ordinary while in the defensive huddle.

"I smelled a cigar while I was in the huddle, and sure enough, I came out of the huddle and there was Pritchett—he had grabbed [sportswriter] Tim Prister's cigar and was puffing away."

"We had as much fun as you could possibly have on the football field," says Stonebreaker. "But we knew when to pull in the reins."

"For me, it was the most fun I ever had on a football field," says Pritchett. "You got to spend four years playing with a great bunch of guys, and you got to represent your alma mater.

"We had a blast...and we won."

Winning was something that Stams and Pritchett didn't take for granted. Each was a fifth-year senior in 1988 after enduring Notre Dame's 5–6 season as freshmen in 1985.

"Having experienced the hard times, we had a deeper appreciation for the success we achieved," says Stams. "It was a pretty good rags-to-riches story."

"That definitely made us appreciate what kind of opportunity we had in 1988," says Pritchett of Notre Dame's rise in the polls as the Irish kept racking up wins.

The Amigos were a huge reason that Notre Dame was able to take advantage of that opportunity and claim its 11th consensus national championship.

Both Stams and Stonebreaker were first-team All-Americans, while Pritchett also earned All-America mention. Stams was at his best in Notre Dame's biggest games, as CBS's Notre Dame Most Valuable Player in the 31–30 win over number one Miami and as the Most Valuable Defensive Player in the Fiesta Bowl win over West Virginia.

All three went on to play in the NFL, but there was something special about Notre Dame's magical 1988 season.

"That whole last year was an experience I'll take with me for the rest of my life," says Pritchett, who has made his mark in the financial world as a licensed bond trader with Bear Stearns. "The things we overcome along the way set a precedent for what you have to do in order to be successful for the rest of your life."

Indeed, from earning spots on NFL rosters to success in the business world, each of the Amigos has continued to enjoy great success.

As the youngest of the three, Stonebreaker had the unique experience of life at Notre Dame without the Amigos. He both missed the other two Amigos and drew on their time together during his final season at Notre Dame.

"All of a sudden I was one of the oldest guys on the team, and it was a different feeling," recalls Stonebreaker, who returned to his native New Orleans as the owner and CEO of NoBrew, a company that offers ice coffee and other specialty coffees in customers' homes.

"The best thing about playing with those guys was competing with each other to get to the ball carrier quickest," he said. "It didn't even matter what the offense was running."

Stonebreaker obviously was getting to a lot of ball carriers in a hurry during 1990, his final season, once again earning first-team All-America honors.

With the birth of Pritchett's son Lawson Kenneth, the Three Amigos have become the three fathers. Stams dotes over his two youngsters, Rhiannon and Mason, while Stonebreaker prepares for the day when he'll be kept busy keeping a future version of the Amigos away from his daughters, Savannah and Violette.

While family responsibilities have kept the Amigos from getting together as often as they'd like, they retain their passion for football—and Notre Dame in particular.

"I watch every game, and I still live, breathe, and die with it," says Pritchett. "And I can't stand it."

Stams, who regales University of Akron football fans with his football knowledge and wit as a commentator on the Zips' radio broadcasts, is reminded of some of the extracurricular activities the Amigos encountered in their day.

"I remember when you went toe-to-toe with that Miami kicker near the tunnel in '88," he taunts Pritchett.

"You didn't expect me to take on one of those big linemen, did you?" responds Pritchett, who backed down from no one in his career.

As the Amigos trade insults, they plan for a mini-reunion at an upcoming Notre Dame game. Thank goodness all three are devoted family men, so the women and children should be safe, but when the Amigos get back together, somebody better lock up the quarterbacks.

Catching Up with...Ned Bolcar

Listening to Ned Bolcar, it would be easy to get the impression that he thinks he was born about 20 years too early.

A native of Phillipsburg, New Jersey, where he was named the *USA Today* National High School Player of the Year as a senior, Bolcar is the quintessential "Jersey Guy" that current Notre Dame head coach Charlie Weis so often exalts. The only trouble is, Bolcar clearly lives his life without regrets—although a few doubts may have crept in during his freshman season at Notre Dame.

A lifelong Irish fan, Bolcar recalls being in Michigan's visiting locker room as a freshman and having a veteran Irish player admonish him to quiet down and "act like [I'd] been there."

Moments later, Bolcar was stretching while the Michigan squad thundered onto the field, "with blood in their eyes and snot bubbles coming out of their noses." Bolcar turned to a fellow freshman and accurately predicted, "We're going to get the tar beat out of us today." Michigan won 20–12.

All that changed a few months later when Lou Holtz took over as Notre Dame's head coach.

"The very first meeting he came into the room and asked one of the seniors how long he had been playing football," Bolcar said. "The player said something like 10 years, and Coach Holtz responded that if the player didn't sit up straight, his career would be over in three seconds. All of a sudden, you heard the sound of a hundred butts hitting the backs of seats."

It was unlikely that Bolcar's was one of those butts requiring a sudden shift—his work ethic may have exceeded his considerable talent. He was a second-team All-American linebacker in 1989, but considers twice being voted Notre Dame tri-captain by his teammates to be an even greater honor.

Bolcar and his teammates produced a national championship in 1988 and 23 straight victories—the greatest stretch in Notre Dame football since the Leahy era.

"I had such great classmates—a bunch of guys who chose Notre Dame not only because they wanted to excel on the football team, but because they wanted to excel at life. And the Notre Dame students are very similar to the football players; they're all very driven."

Bolcar, a second-team All-American in 1987 and 1989, when he led the Irish in tackles with 106 and 109, respectively, played two years in the NFL. He recalls his first meeting with Weis: "He didn't talk to me about Xs and Os, he talked to me about needing to get players who get it."

Bolcar, who obviously "got it," is finding an outlet for his competitive fires in institutional equities sales for the Wall Street firm of Jefferies and Company. "There are lots of type-A personalities here," he laughs.

Bolcar's future plans still include raising a family.

"When they bury you, they're not going to say he was an NFL player or a great Notre Dame football player; I want them to say he was a great husband, a great father, a great man."

Catching Up with...Tim Grunhard

When Tim Grunhard retired after 11 seasons as a Pro Bowl center with the Kansas City Chiefs, he thought his life would get easier.

Sure, Grunhard still had his daily radio show in his adopted hometown of Kansas City, and he is very involved in raising four young children—C.J., twins Cailey and Colin, and Cassie—with his wife, Sarah. Even Grunhard's commitment to civic activity on top of everything else would leave time for more leisurely pursuits.

Little did Grunhard realize that somewhere along the line he caught the coaching bug. After a stint as a high school assistant, Grunhard was the offensive line coach with the Cologne Centurions in NFL Europe for one season. He loved the experience professionally, and the entire family enjoyed the time abroad, but Grunhard also realized that the time demands were just too great, given the ages of his children.

But when Bishop Miege High School in suburban Kansas City needed a new head football coach following the 2005 season, Grunhard couldn't resist. And although he parlayed hard work into success on football's biggest stages, Grunhard's primary objective is producing solid young men—not necessarily professional football players.

"I have played for some great coaches over the years," Grunhard notes, "and it's always been a passion of mine to share the experiences and the fundamentals that helped me.

"I know that most of these players aren't going to go on to play at Notre Dame or in the NFL, but our goal is to put them out into the community as better people."

The Bishop Miege football program had struggled in recent years, a situation that's hardly unfamiliar to Grunhard.

He was a member of Lou Holtz's first Notre Dame recruiting class, arriving in the immediate aftermath of Gerry Faust's final 5–6 season. By the time he was a junior, Grunhard was a starting guard on Notre Dame's 1988 national championship team. Over his last two seasons, the Irish were 24–1.

"It's a mind-set, a confidence, a belief," explains Grunhard about rebuilding a program. "You have to walk onto the field expecting to win."

Listening to Grunhard, Holtz's influence is impossible to miss, especially when he speaks of his emphasis on "love, trust, and commitment," staples of the soon-to-be-Hall-of-Fame coach's philosophy.

While Grunhard names playing for Holtz, winning a national championship, and earning his degree as life-changing experiences while at Notre Dame, even those take a backseat on his list.

"The best thing that ever happened to me was finding my wife there," he says.

Catching Up with...Reggie Brooks

By the end of his sophomore year at Notre Dame, Reggie Brooks was ready to come home. The Tulsa, Oklahoma, native had followed in the footsteps of his brother, Tony, by spurning overtures from local universities to play at Notre Dame.

But while Tony had earned significant playing time as a freshman in 1987 and was a star on Notre Dame's 1988 national championship team, Reggie had yet to enjoy similar success. Brooks had already informed the Notre Dame and Oklahoma State University coaches of his intention to transfer and play for the Cowboys.

There was just one more person Brooks had to talk to, his father, Raymond.

"He said that I was going to finish what I started, and that I was going to stay at Notre Dame," recalls Brooks.

After one more season of biding his time, Reggie made Notre Dame fans very grateful that Raymond Brooks halted those transfer plans. As a senior in 1992, Reggie had one of the most amazing seasons in Notre Dame history. He rushed for 1,343 yards on 8.04 yards per carry, second only to George Gipp's 1920 mark of 8.10 in the Notre Dame record book.

Brooks announced his presence to the college football world in spectacular fashion against Michigan in Notre Dame Stadium.

His spinning, whirling 20-yard touchdown run through five Wolverine would-be tacklers was ESPN's Play of the Year. The phenomenal effort left Brooks nearly unconscious and without any recollection of the play.

When Brooks saw the run on film, he was as incredulous as everybody else.

"I did that?" Brooks remembers thinking.

Reggie Brooks's 1992 average of 8.04 yards per carry ranks second on Notre Dame's all-time list only to George Gipp's record of 8.10 in 1920.

It truly was an unbelievable season, as Brooks ended his season by finishing fifth in the 1992 Heisman Trophy balloting—no Irish player would make the top five again until Brady Quinn in 2005.

In an ironic twist, the young man who was ready to put South Bend in his rearview mirror for good has returned to Notre Dame. Back in Tulsa after playing several seasons in the National Football League, Reggie and his wife, Christina, were talking about where they wanted to raise their four children—daughters Aespyne and Rayna and sons Alex and Gabe.

Just a few weeks later, Brooks received a call about a vacancy in the university's Office of Information Technologies (he also does commentary on Notre Dame football for Notre Dame Sports Properties shows).

"I enjoy working with computers, and I enjoy working with people," says Brooks. "It's great to be back."

Cheerios Remark Tough to Stomach for Holtz

Notre Dame was headed to the 1992 Sugar Bowl to play Florida, but that didn't mean the Irish—losers of two of their last three games in the regular season—didn't have their detractors. In Orlando, Florida, for the holidays, head coach Lou Holtz was greeted in a T.G.I. Friday's restaurant by this joke from his waiter: "What's the difference between Notre Dame and Cheerios? Cheerios belong in a bowl." Holtz milked the line for all it was worth—and he had the last laugh. His Irish beat the third-rated Florida Gators 39–28.

How did Notre Dame pull it off? Normally more at home calling plays, Holtz stuck his fingers into the defensive scheme and decided to disdain the pass rush and drop more people into coverage. That strategy seemed to bamboozle Gators coach Steve Spurrier and quarterback Shane Matthews. Florida finished with 511 total yards, but the Gators had to settle for five field goals.

Behind 16–7 at halftime, the Irish went for their power running game after intermission, and Jerome Bettis ended up with 150 ground yards (127 in the second half) and three touchdowns in the fourth period. Notre Dame ran for 245 yards in the second half, while Florida went 53 minutes between touchdowns.

What was waiting in the Irish football offices when the team returned from New Orleans? A case of Cheerios.

Catching Up with...Rick Mirer

It all unfolded so rapidly, fueled by a great sense of urgency. But as the years have passed, Rick Mirer's memories of the final game he played in Notre Dame Stadium have become crystal clear.

The opponent was Penn State, in the November 14, 1992, classic, which immediately became known in Notre Dame lore as the "Snow Bowl."

Played in a swirling snowstorm, the game hadn't gone particularly well for the high-powered Notre Dame offense. The Irish had yet to score a touchdown when they got the ball with 4:19 to play, trailing 16–9.

Mirer led the Irish downfield, but with 25 seconds remaining, it was fourth and goal from the Penn State 3. The touchdown came relatively easy, as Mirer hit a wide-open Jerome Bettis, pulling the Irish to within one point.

Notre Dame head coach Lou Holtz decided on a two-point conversion. Working with an empty backfield, Mirer patiently waited. And waited. He finally scrambled to his right and spotted 5'8" tailback Reggie Brooks—owner of one of the most spectacular rushing seasons in Notre Dame history, but just one pass reception—drifting toward the right corner of the end zone.

Mirer lofted the ball over a rapidly closing Penn State lineman and it sailed high toward the shortest player on the field. With fans tightly packed around the perimeter of the field, some in the press box were unable to see whether Brooks snared the pass.

Mirer didn't have to wait for the crowd's delirious eruption to learn whether his pass had found its mark.

"I knew he was going to catch it," says the former All-American quarterback, who still ranks third on Notre Dame's career total offense list. "Reggie's effort was what that whole drive was all about.

"It wasn't the prettiest game on offense, although our defense played great. Sometimes, you just need to have your back to the wall. We had one shot, and that was it.

"We played some great rivals, but in a lot of ways, Penn State was most like us—with the plain uniforms, a cold-weather team, and very tough. What a great way to end our careers. If it had been a bad throw, it would have been a sick feeling—forever."

Mirer went on to spend over a decade in the NFL, and now lives near San Diego with his wife, Stephanie, and sons, Morrison, Oliver, and Charlie. Since his playing days ended, Mirer travels with his family and is involved in a start-up sports venture.

As a hotly pursued high school recruit from Goshen, Indiana, Mirer picked Notre Dame over Michigan and many others. The 40-mile distance to South Bend allowed frequent visits while in high school. "I felt like I fit in really well," he remembers.

Now, more than 2,000 miles away, little has changed. "No matter how many new buildings they build, it still feels like home," he says.

Catching Up with…Kevin McDougal

"It was just a matter of time."

So says Kevin McDougal, who seemingly came out of nowhere to quarterback Notre Dame to an 11–1 season in 1993.

Seven days after dethroning number one Florida State, undefeated Notre Dame trailed Boston College 38–17 with 11:13 left in the game.

Indeed, it was just a matter of time; the Irish didn't have enough. McDougal thought otherwise.

He produced arguably the greatest comeback in Notre Dame history. Neither the Ice Bowl (1979 Cotton Bowl) nor the Snow Bowl (1992 against Penn State) held such high stakes. And the 1935 Ohio State game involved a smaller deficit.

As Irish head coach Lou Holtz noted, this comeback was unique in that it wasn't fueled by the defense. McDougal led the Irish on touchdown drives of 57 and 67 yards to get to 38–32.

Notre Dame got the ball one last time on its 34-yard line with 2:51 remaining. Five plays later, it came down to one snap—fourth-and-goal on the Boston College 4.

Holtz asked McDougal what play he wanted. McDougal eschewed the playbook. He simply told every receiver to flood the end zone and keep moving.

Just before he was leveled, McDougal shot Lake Dawson a laser in the back of the end zone, knee high and barely out of the reach of a defender. The extra point made it 39–38 Notre Dame.

But, again, it was a matter of time. McDougal had left *too* much time. David Gordon's 41-yard field goal as time expired handed the top-rated Irish a heartwrenching 41–39 loss.

McDougal's signature moment, for all its brilliance, was written in erasable ink.

For McDougal, who still holds Notre Dame's all-time career record for highest pass completion percentage, just getting a chance to play quarterback was another "matter of time."

Stuck behind three-year starter Rick Mirer, McDougal finally got his chance as a senior. To say that McDougal made the most of his long-awaited opportunity is an understatement.

McDougal credits his teammates and especially his parents for encouraging and preparing him to excel when given the chance.

After a long and successful career playing quarterback in several professional leagues, McDougal is embarking in the business world while also attempting to encourage youngsters with his message of persistence.

Asked to provide a bumper-sticker-sized description of his Notre Dame career, McDougal says simply, "He really cared."

McDougal's play left no doubt as to that.

Catching Up with...Devon McDonald

At 6'4", 241 pounds, Devon McDonald had a profound impact on the football field. The native of Jamaica, by way of Paterson, New Jersey, was the most outstanding defensive player in the final game he ever played for Notre Dame, a 28–3 victory over Texas A&M in the 1993 Cotton Bowl.

Today, McDonald is having an even greater impact on thousands of young people as a part of Sports World Inc., an organization whose mission is "to send professional athletes to share personal life experiences with students, helping them to recognize the consequences of their choices while challenging them with the message of hope."

Notwithstanding his stellar career at Notre Dame and four seasons in the NFL, there was a time in McDonald's life when he was far from happy about the consequences flowing from the choices he was making.

Eventually McDonald experienced "an epiphany," as he describes it. "It was clear that I didn't want to live anymore and I knew I was about to make a life-changing decision," he relates. "Sure, I had made the NFL, but I had nothing because I found out that money didn't buy me what I needed.

"It was at that time that I received Christ and He became a reality in my life," says McDonald. "I invited Him to come into my heart, and that began my transformation."

As his faith grew, McDonald was confronted with questions about how he would live his life.

"Once I decided to give my life to Christ, I had to figure out, 'What am I going to do?'" he recalls. "I had to figure out, 'Am I going to do more than make money?'"

Shortly after he began to pray about the decisions he faced, McDonald received a telephone call from Steve Grant, a friend and former West Virginia football player who had become involved with Sports World. McDonald accepted Grant's invitation to join Sports World.

Now an ordained minister, McDonald is convinced that his own struggles allow him to be effective with the young people he encounters.

"First of all, it's my relationship with Christ," McDonald explains. "Beyond that, I believe what I'm saying, and people can sense that, especially young people.

"I know what it feels like to be hopeless," he says.

McDonald shared his encounter with a young woman who showed him cuts on her arms, cuts she had made in an attempt to kill herself because somebody told her she was fat and ugly. After hearing McDonald's message, the woman described to him a newfound sense of hope.

"Words are powerful," McDonald observes. "If you can speak a word of hope into a hungry soul, you can revive it."

McDonald lives with his wife, Shereasher, and daughters, Jazzmine and Rachel, near the Sports World headquarters in Indianapolis. He encourages those interested in supporting Sports World or bringing a Sports World representative to their local to school to visit the organization's website at www.sportsworld.org.

chapter 9
The Bob Davie Years

After serving as defensive coordinator for three seasons under Lou Holtz, Bob Davie was awarded Notre Dame's head coaching position in November 1996.

Bob Davie's initial season as Notre Dame head coach in 1997 included a victory in Baton Rouge against the 11th-ranked Tigers, in which the Irish, for the first time in history, played a football game without a turnover or a penalty. The Irish won 24–6.

Yesterday's Heroes: Kory Minor

"Of those to whom much is given, much is expected."
—Luke 12:48

At the Friday night pep rally before Kory Minor's final home game against LSU in 1998, Minor's mother, Kim, walked to the podium and surprised her son and the capacity Joyce Center crowd with a moving "thank you" to the Notre Dame community for taking care of Kory during his four-year stay at the university.

In the first row of players' seats, with tears of pride slowly streaming from his eyes to his cheeks, Minor carefully listened in appreciation of the moment he was experiencing. Less than four years earlier, Kim Brown-Minor accompanied Kory on his recruiting visit to campus where the pair first became enamored with Notre Dame. That night her son's journey was nearly complete.

The Notre Dame community did watch over Minor, graduating a student who was respected on campus as much for his concern for others and the Christian faith as for any gridiron statistic, cheering on a team captain and all-time sacks leader who enjoyed a four-year career with the Carolina Panthers before retirement in 2003, and educating a marketing major who returned home to Southern California and embarked on a livelihood as a wine consultant for the E.&J. Gallo Winery.

But by the time he first set foot on campus, Minor had already received a lifetime's worth of guidance from his mother.

"She is a person who gave her whole life to her children," says Minor. "All the late nights talking about homework, family, and games—she was a woman of many hats for me. The knowledge I learned from her and the love I have for her is truly priceless."

As a single parent, Kim successfully raised her son Kory and daughter Koi, who was a high school senior in 2006–2007 and a nationally recognized basketball standout.

Today, mother and son live just miles apart in suburban Los Angeles. Kim teaches in Head Start, a child development program designed to assist children and pregnant women in families with low income, in Colton. Kory and his wife, Lisa, "nearly" high school sweethearts who met on graduation day at Bishop Amat Memorial High School and dated while classmates at Notre Dame, have a young daughter, Ilyanna, and reside in Moreno Valley.

More importantly, though, Minor's mother continues to provide the example by which her son treats others. Just as he served the South Bend community as a Notre Dame student, Minor volunteers in the Los Angeles community as a speaker in area schools and with his mother's Head Start group.

"I get to know everybody I come across," says Minor. "I was always a person who cared about people and their well-being. I hope to be the one who brightens up a room with my laughter and smile."

Because of all that he has been given, Minor adheres to the notion that much is expected.

A good mother still means everything.

Kory Minor looks over the Michigan defense on September 5, 1998, when the Irish defeated the Wolverines, 36–20. Photo courtesy of Getty Images/Jonathon Daniel.

Catching Up with...Jim Sanson

Imagine a moment so powerful that it can convince your mind that it is silent, even though more than 80,000 people are screaming at you.

That's just how former Notre Dame kicker Jim Sanson describes the seconds leading up to a game-winning field-goal attempt.

Irish head coach Lou Holtz sent the freshman into the cauldron against Texas in 1996. Sanson silenced the Longhorn faithful by kicking a 39-yard field goal as time expired to lift Notre Dame over number six Texas 27–24. It was one of three last-minute, game-winning kicks for Sanson, whose 28 career field goals leave him in sixth place on Notre Dame's all-time list.

During his junior season, he produced game-winning field goals against Purdue with 57 seconds remaining in a 31–30 comeback victory and knocked through the decisive points when he hit a career-long 47-yarder versus Army with 1:06 left to give the Irish a 20–17 victory.

Every kicker's life is marked by ups and downs. Sanson learned to persevere—and keep a suitcase packed at all times.

During one week following a missed kick, Sanson wasn't allowed a single kick in practice. He assumed that meant he had lost his job, only to have Holtz bark at him as the traveling team was boarding its buses to the next game.

"Son, where's your bag?"

Sanson found time as a student to establish Notre Dame Athletes Against Drugs, which grew to include 140 Notre Dame athletes working in South Bend to help keep children away from illegal drugs. He graduated from the College of Arts and Letters in May 2000 with a degree in economics.

Today, Sanson is vice president of The Athlete's Agency, a Southern California business that coordinates public appearances for athletes and sports celebrities.

"I love what I do and it's unbelievable how much being from Notre Dame has helped me in this business."

Football Alumni Strap It on One More Time

A group of former Notre Dame football players traveled to Hamburg, Germany, to play against a German team, the Hamburg Blue Devils, in Charity Bowl VIII. The game took place on July 8, 2000, at Volksparkstadion. These diary entries comprise the story of their weeklong attempt to "wake up the echoes."

They didn't complain a bit.

In fact, the Notre Dame football players who hit the practice field in the first day of preparation for their Charity Bowl meeting with the Hamburg Blue Devils seemed to enjoy every moment of their two hours of work on a pleasant, 70-degree afternoon.

Remember, there were more than a few members of this Notre Dame alumni football squad who hadn't put on pads or helmets for some years. The veterans on the team were 1976 tight end Al Bucci and '71 quarterback Pat Steenberge. Others, like Reggie Brooks and Pat Eilers, weren't long out of the National Football League (in Brooks's case, Barcelona of NFL Europe, as well). Likewise, with Adrian Jarrell and the Arena Football League.

The consensus seemed to be that of Darnell Smith as the first practice commenced: "I feel like I've never taken this uniform off."

There were a few muscles asked to respond for the first time in a while. Offensive lineman Mike Perrino moved slowly, trying to keep his back in order. Defensive lineman Bryan Flannery suffered a groin injury early in the workout. Meanwhile, Brooks and fellow tailback Lee Becton wasted little time displaying flashes of their 1,000-yard seasons with the Irish. Brooks, in particular, seemed to be in midseason form. Veteran linebacker Wes Pritchett intercepted a pass during the pass skeleton series, spiked the football, and showed the same enthusiasm that made him one of the emotional leaders of the '88 Irish national title team.

Remember, too, that some of these Notre Dame players know each other by name only. Quarterback Steve Belles shook hands with center Greg Stec as they began working on quarterback-center exchanges early in the workout.

The appearance of a Notre Dame football squad drew a half-dozen photographers to the workout. Helped by exposure in Germany from NBC Sports telecasts of Irish home games, names like Brooks, Becton, and Kris Haines—who caught the last-second touchdown pass from Joe Montana in the '79 Cotton Bowl—were more than a little familiar to the hometown journalists. An NFL Films crew appeared at one practice and the local Hamburg newspapers featured color photos from practice, impressive coverage for a nonsoccer event, according to German officials.

Off the field, the Notre Dame group enjoyed an evening boat trip through the Hamburg canals, complete with noisemakers and confetti for the Fourth of July.

Another interesting perspective came from the sons of former players like Perrino, Ron Plantz, Pat Kramer, and Jack Shields, all of whom attended practice. The boys had heard their dads talk about playing football for Notre Dame but obviously had never seen what that really meant. On game day, the sons will watch the fathers put on those gold helmets and blue jerseys one more time—and it's hard to tell who's looking forward to it more.

When the Irish arrived for practice (in helmets and shorts only, no pads), they found a handmade sign draped over fences enclosing the practice field area. It read, *"Wieso zeight Ihr der WELT nicht das Ihr die Blue Devils seit und nicht die Blue Deppen,"* which, translated loosely, said, "Let's show the world we're the Blue Devils, not the Blue Dummies." That's in reference to some recent newspaper headlines describing the recent Blue Devil on-field struggles.

Injured inside linebacker Dave Butler (who couldn't play due to a broken foot) was invited to lead the team in 10 jumping jacks. He complied, on one foot.

Notre Dame officials who attended the Blue Devils' 26–14 loss the previous week to the Munich Cowboys said the noise level amongst fans was intense, even with a crowd of around 6,000. With an expected crowd of 25,000 to 30,000 for the Notre Dame game, Irish coaches are anticipating a wild scene.

Irish quarterback Tony Rice is here, even though he can't play due to surgery for a torn Achilles tendon suffered in the flag football warm-up game in April. He's a familiar name to German fans based on his former involvement with the Munich team in the European League.

Likely starters for the Irish on defense are Brian Hamilton, Corey Bennett, Melvin Dansby, and Andre Jones up front, Karl McGill at outside linebacker, and Wes Pritchett and Jeremy Sample inside—and Ivory Covington, Ty Goode, Brandy Wells, and Pat Eilers in the secondary.

Irish team physician Dr. Pat Leary one day donned a helmet and jersey and worked out with the kickers.

Sponsorship is routine in the German Football League. The Hamburg team jerseys feature logos of Holsten Pilsner (a beer company) and Jaxx.de (an Internet company), plus the Ford logo appears prominently on the front of the Blue Devil helmets.

The Blue Devils normally wear a medium blue jersey for home games, but they will wear white since Notre Dame is identified best by its home blue jerseys.

Former Notre Dame players relived the glory one last time when they suited up to play a memorable exhibition game in Hamburg, Germany, in 2000.

Practice sessions have been spirited but somewhat light in tone. With the number of players from the Lou Holtz era (and with son Skip running the offense) there have been more than a few Lou Holtz imitations heard on the practice fields.

The Irish family and friends one day took a two-hour bus trip for a tour of Schwerin Castle. The Irish another night saw the musical *Buddy Holly*, with songs in English and dialogue in German, following a boat tour of the Hamburg harbor.

The conservative newspaper *Hamburgr Abendblatt* featured a color photo of tailback Reggie Brooks. One edition of the *Hamburg Bild* included action shots of Irish players from their college days, with headlines noting their current jobs. So Germans learned about Reggie Brooks, der Computer-Freak; Lee Becton, der Manager; and Terry Andrysiak, der Bank-Prasident.

Real-time stats will be available for the game at www.H-D-B.de (kickoff converts to a noon EST start).

Notre Dame defensive coordinator Greg Mattison and former Irish linebacker Wes Pritchett provided some humor while making comments at a joint barbecue featuring players and administrators from the Notre Dame contingent and the Hamburg Blue Devils. Mattison, who was serving as the official representative of the current Irish coaching staff, shared his observations from the recent practice sessions.

"A lot of these players have no idea what will happen in there when the game rolls around, and for a coach that's a little bit scary," Mattison said. "You see a guy like Wes Pritchett running down the field and you hope he gets a little faster by Saturday night." Pritchett—who clearly hasn't lost his trademark sense of humor or willingness for public speaking—later followed up on Mattison's comments while addressing the gathering.

"You have to realize that even during my playing days at Notre Dame, back in 1988, that's as fast as I ever ran. So I really haven't become any slower," Pritchett deadpanned.

The Irish worked out in shorts for an hour the morning before the game, with final on-field preparation consisting of a walk-through of all the Notre Dame offenses, defenses, and special teams.

Serving as captains of the Irish team are tailback Mark Green and safety Pat Eilers.

The Notre Dame party attended a coat-and-tie reception one evening for the game charity, Kinder helfen Kindern. *Hamburger Abendblatt*, the city's conservative newspaper, served as host for the reception after featuring the game in a special section of one edition of its paper. Representing Notre Dame on the speaking program was former cornerback D'Juan Francisco, who impressed guests by making his remarks in German. That earned Francisco a chance the next day to lead the team in jumping jacks, calling out numbers from one to 10 in German at practice. Francisco had not originally been expected to play because of injuries, but he now at least should suit up.

Former defensive end Frank Stams, an '88 All-American, arrived in Hamburg two days before the game to spend some time with many of his former teammates. Doctors advised him not to play, but there's some possibility he may yet suit up.

Former Irish defensive back Mike Haywood, now on the LSU staff, has been handling the Notre Dame special teams.

The offensive team that opened practice featured Terry Andrysiak at quarterback, Mark Green at tailback, Dean Lytle at fullback, Mike Denvir at tight end, Emmett Mosley and Clint Johnson at wide receiver, Mike Perrino and Jim Kordas at tackle, Tom Freeman and Ron Plantz at guard, and Rick Kaczenski at center. Look for Lee Becton and Clint Johnson deep for kickoff returns.

The game will feature four 12-minute periods.

The Hamburg team normally practices from 7:00 to 9:00 P.M. on Tuesday, Wednesday, and Thursday. Most players work full-time jobs during the day and some commute from as far as 70 miles away for practice.

Original plans called for the Notre Dame team to line up by jersey number and be introduced individually before the game, but the Irish coaches opted for the more traditional en masse entrance.

After the game, both teams will line up along the sidelines and end lines, join hands, and salute the crowd as part of a German tradition.

Notre Dame coaches have been told to expect WWF-style introductions and entrances for the Hamburg team, as well as nonstop music throughout the game—potentially making audibles difficult. The Blue Devils also sponsor multiple groups of cheerleaders, all of whom will be present for the game.

Former Notre Dame quarterback Don White (1957 to 1959), father of Irish assistant Brian White, made the trip and has been assisting with the Notre Dame linebackers.

The two teams attended a joint dinner the night before the game at Volksparkstadion, with players exchanging gifts.

Notre Dame team chaplain Rev. James Riehle, C.S.C., was featured in the tabloid *Hamburger Morgan Post*, under a headline that suggested he was the Fighting Irish representative with the best connections to the top.

The German football magazine *Huddle* appeared on newsstands, with its cover featuring artwork of the Notre Dame team heading down the Notre Dame Stadium tunnel and the interior including biographies of all the Notre Dame players.

The awarding of the soccer World Cup to Germany made the front page of all the German papers after the announcement two days prior to the game.

Hamburg Blue Devil assistant coach Jeff Reinebold, who also works with the team's administration, is a South Bend native. His father, Jim, is currently a coach with the Class A South Bend Silver Hawks minor league baseball team after a long career as baseball coach at South Bend Clay High School—and his mother, Evelyn, formerly worked in the housing office at the University of Notre Dame.

* * *

The game started about 15 minutes late, as afternoon rain slowed down the pregame pageantry. There were some 400 cheerleaders surrounding the field throughout the game. Game-time temperatures were in the 50s. Just prior to Notre Dame taking the field, a six-minute video highlighting Notre Dame football was shown on the big screen at one end of the stadium. The Irish entered the field to a standing ovation and fireworks. Leprechaun

Michael Brown was in attendance for the game. The boisterous atmosphere was helped by recorded music that played throughout the game.

When it came to the game itself, it couldn't have been scripted any better. That was the consensus after Notre Dame's alumni football team utilized a game-saving end zone interception by Ivory Covington on the final play to hold off the Hamburg Blue Devils 14–10 in front of a noisy crowd of 18,500 at Volksparkstadion in Hamburg.

The Irish overcame two early missed field goals and a 3–0 deficit as Steve Belles rushed for one score and threw for another to give the Irish a 14–3 lead midway through the final period. But the Blue Devils roared back, scoring a touchdown with just more than four minutes remaining—and they were knocking on the door again as the final play unfolded with 0.9 seconds left on the clock.

That's when Covington made a diving end zone interception as the Hamburg team ran its final play on a second-and-goal situation from the Irish 7.

"I thought we had you guys," said Blue Devils defensive end Tuli Mateialona in the joint press conference after the game. "It must have been the luck of the Irish."

"Watch out for those little leprechauns," said Irish tailback Reggie Brooks, who was selected the Notre Dame MVP by the Blue Devils' fan club and received a trophy during the press conference.

"The whole atmosphere was electric," said Blue Devils assistant Jeff Reinebold. "The way the Notre Dame players were jumping around, I don't think the game was any less important to them than when they won the national championship in 1988."

Neither team had much success running the football, with the Irish netting only 47 yards on the ground and the Blue Devils managing only 52. Brooks paced the Irish with 46 yards on 13 carries, including a key 14-yard gain on a third-down play in the final minutes.

Irish starter Terry Andrysiak threw for 129 yards. Belles came off the bench and hit a 50-yard bomb to Clint Johnson on his first throw of the night, setting up his own two-yard option keeper on third down.

Notre Dame began by driving 48 yards in 10 plays to start the game, before Ted Gradel's 39-yard field goal came up just short. Andrysiak completed his first three passes of the game for a combined 28 yards. Then, Hamburg came right back, using a 51-yard passing gain to set itself up at the Irish 14 where Andreas Lefevre connected from 31 yards for a 3–0 Blue Devils lead.

The Irish fumbled the football away on their next series after a 59-yard throw from Andrysiak to Adrian Jarrell took Notre Dame to the Blue Devils 9. To start the second period, the Irish missed out on a 13-play march that reached the Hamburg 8, when Gradel missed left from 35 yards out. It was Ty Goode's interception near midfield that set up the first Notre Dame points, with Belles hitting Johnson for 44 on the next play.

The two teams traded fumbles early in the third period, and a second Irish recovery after a Blue Devils pass completion set up Notre Dame at the Hamburg 36. This time Belles hit Johnson for a 23-yard touchdown play to make it 14–3.

The final Hamburg points came on a 49-yard drive, the last 31 on a pass from Matt Wyatt, a former Mississippi State quarterback, to Che Johnson, who played at New Mexico.

Two Brooks runs for 14 yards each gained first downs for Notre Dame. But the Irish finally had to punt, and Hamburg took over with 1:33 left on its own 47. Wyatt's passing put the Blue Devils within striking distance, but Covington ended the suspense a moment later.

Said Reinebold after the game, "A lot of people thought this game would never happen. They laughed when it was suggested. What you saw today will probably never happen again on this continent."

One More Golden Moment

On July 8, 2000, in Volksparkstadion in Hamburg, Germany, a team of Notre Dame alumni football players met the Hamburg Blue Devils in Charity Bowl VIII. The Fighting Irish team was represented by players who had seen varsity action over the past 30 years in South Bend, Indiana, and wherever this historic team traveled.

Many of them had played in the National Football League, a handful were All-Americans, and there were numerous team captains—but all had given up the game some years prior to putting on the pads one more time in Germany. This game was for charity, for friendship, and for a rekindling of the spirit that is truly unique to Notre Dame football. I happened to be the elder statesman of this team, and just happy to be out there with the rest of the guys, throwing the ball and trying to get us on the scoreboard.

Pat Steenberge #11
Class of '73

*   *   *

"Pass 52 Race, on one Pass 52 Race, on one—ready, break!"

As I head to the line of scrimmage it all seems so familiar, yet so surrealistic. Is this real or fantasy?

My mind races through a well-memorized checklist in the three seconds or so until I reach under center to start the cadence. Get the snap, reverse pivot, good hand fake, eyes into his stomach, he'll be open—just wait for things to open up, touchdown coming, hang it out there so the receiver can run under it, this will be complete...

"Set" (got to yell louder with those blasted whistles blowing).

"Blue-11, Blue-11" (perfect—the safety is creeping up to support the run).

"Hike."

The snap is hard and clean. I step back with my left foot to 6:00, ball into my stomach just like I learned in fourth grade, here comes the tailback, whoa, something on my right foot, falling down, on the ground, whistle blows, fourth down.

As I jog to the sideline, a very long way, as I recall, to the questioning eyes of the coach, I wonder what just happened. Why did I go down? Did a lineman get pushed back onto me? Did I simply stumble on my own? That's a distinct possibility since it was 29 years ago that I last played real football. No, surely I got tripped.

But I wanted so badly to complete that pass. We could have iced the game with a score, gone up by 18 points, and I would be a star again.

The festive crowd of 19,000 fanatical Germans is still rockin', the music is still blaring as if I am at Woodstock, whistles are screeching, but disappointment sinks deeply into my gut as I try to explain what happened to NFL Europe coach Peter Vaas, our quarterbacks coach for this alumni game.

Catching a sip of water, strange memories haunt me. This is all too reminiscent of Purdue in a downpour that September afternoon of 1971, when an errant snap got buried in the mud at the 1-yard line, and the Boilermakers recovered. The same trek to the sideline, Ara looking bewildered, my teammates distraught as time was running short and we continued to trail 7–0.

Now, our very veteran team, whose average age is well over 30 years, will have to hold on with older legs but with the same battle-honed determination that has been a trademark of Fighting Irish teams since Rockne. We have players here who were trained by Parseghian, Devine, Faust, Holtz, and Davie, who have stood up to USC, Michigan, Penn State, Florida State, and all the others who would make their seasons by defeating Notre Dame.

Hamburg mounts a drive, aided by a mysterious fourth-down interference call that ignites them and gives them relief. Touchdown, Blue Devils! Now this is all too dramatic, as we only lead by four points with too much time left in the fourth quarter. Why couldn't we have gotten a few first downs and run the clock some?

Terry Andrysiak, a solid, confident quarterback, leads the offense back out, but after one first down we have to punt again. With less than one minute to play the Volksparkstadion is in utter chaos. It seems there are 100,000 fans here, and they are witnessing an unbelievable finish to the 1,000th game (does this really count?) in the storied history of Notre Dame football. If this is not just a wonderful dream, the first Notre Dame game of the 21st century is going down to the wire.

Our defense is gritty but certainly weary. Our wonderful hosts this week made sure that we were softened up by the bowl-like atmosphere of boat rides, July 4 celebrations, press conferences, dinner-musicals, and a generally grand time each night. Hamburg has not attempted to run the ball in two quarters, relying on a passing game a la Florida State. Why do they have to play that cursed Seminole Indian soundtrack whenever the Blue Devils complete a pass?

Twenty seconds remain, a long fade into the corner where a Hamburg receiver is open; at the last moment Ty Goode leaps and tips it away.

There is a confident tension on the sideline, as we have all been here before. For the members of the '88 national championship team, which form the nucleus of this alumni team, they clearly expect to be victorious over all odds. The rest of us do, also, especially against a team from another country, and regardless of our individual ages.

Eight seconds left, pass into the middle of the end zone, and Pat Eilers reaches up to bat it down.

For alumni head coach and current Irish defensive coordinator Greg Mattison, this is a defining moment, where both legend and reality tell us that Notre Dame men always can dig deeper. He relates this to his squad during the last timeout.

But, does Wes Pritchett at 34 years, an All-American 12 years ago, possessing unquestionable will to win, still have anything left? Do Melvin Dansby, Brian Hamilton, and George Marshall, all brilliant players in their day but whose best football is years behind them, have one more total effort of four seconds of action to give?

Shotgun formation, snap, roll left, throw left and low into the end zone. Interception! Ivory Covington, we win 14–10.

The players and staff rush onto the field in mayhem as if we had just defeated Texas in the Cotton Bowl. There is hugging, grasping, hooting, embracing, savoring a spectacular completion to a truly unbelievable week. The simple innocence of youth returns for a fleeting moment, and the thrill of victory overwhelms each of us as the fireworks explode around the stadium.

About 45 minutes later the team assembles again in the locker room, having received the Jim Thorpe Trophy, accolades from the adoring spectators, and heartfelt congratulations from each Hamburg Blue Devils player and coach. We've also saluted each section of fans together, holding hands, Germans and Americans, paying tribute to their loyalty, and as tradition would have it, one final golden helmet salute behind our bench to the Notre Dame faithful.

Presents are given to some of our hosts who treated us as well as any bowl committee had done. Axel Gernert, Hamburg owner and the person most responsible for making this dream come true, is praised for his faith and commitment to the Charity Bowl. Coach Skip Holtz, whose father over a decade of wins and losses had molded many of these somewhat graying men into champions, leads the squad in a rousing version of the greatest fight song of them all, the Notre Dame "Victory March."

As I hesitatingly shed my helmet, cleats, blue jersey, shoulder pads, and stretch socks for what certainly now would be the last time, my mind blurrily races over the moments of the past six days in Germany. If only I could stop action each of those days on the practice field with the guys, the nightly dinners and laughter, the afternoon tours with such silly jokes, the one-for-all feeling amongst this very special gang of once great players but still great people.

Removing the thigh pads and knee pads from the gold pants, I carefully slip out the medals Father Riehle had provided us in a time-honored tradition of the pregame Mass. I had requested and received four, one for each knee and each thigh. They worked!

Center Rick Kaczenski, a trim 25 years young who had graduated from Erie Cathedral Prep only a quarter century after I had, came over and apologized for getting knocked onto me during the fourth quarter, causing the busted play. We laughed aloud and high-fived one another as I felt relieved to know it was not just my 48-year-old clumsiness that had caused the loss.

In the misty dawn, I ambled along the serene Lake Aubenalster in downtown Hamburg, having celebrated a final good-bye with this remarkable group of Notre Dame men, along with an amazing bunch of new German friends. It is now time to return to the beautiful reality that is my family and home in Texas. I am thankful for all my blessings as never before, clinging to a renewed understanding of just what makes Notre Dame so unique and special, and what separates football from all other types of sports…the people.

Just in case you don't remember, we beat Purdue 8-7 in 1971.

chapter 10
The Supporting Cast

After coming across the quote in an old book about Fighting Irish football, Lou Holtz had this sign installed on the wall leading onto the field at Notre Dame Stadium. Photo courtesy of AP/Wide World Images.

Thanks to the NBC Sports television camera that shows Irish players headed down the tunnel to the field at Notre Dame Stadium, the "Play Like a Champion" sign in the Irish locker room has become particularly identified with the Notre Dame football program.

Green Is Good for Brazo and Irish

Most homeowners today take special pride in their backyards, and Dan Brazo is no exception. It just so happens that his backyard measures 120 yards long and 53 yards wide and is surrounded by more than 80,000 seats.

Brazo is the athletics facilities manager at Notre Dame, and one of his primary responsibilities is the maintenance of one of college football's greatest shrines—Notre Dame Stadium. Through the fickle climate changes of South Bend, Brazo and his dedicated crew of eight meticulously work to make sure the stadium turf and grandstands remain as pristine as they were the day the stadium opened more than 75 years ago.

"It's a very humbling experience for me and my crew to work here at Notre Dame Stadium," Brazo says.

"This is the best job in the world," he says, "and one of the more difficult aspects of it is to make sure it doesn't just become routine. We can't lose sight of what this place stands for and what it all means."

Maintaining a stadium of any size can be a daunting task. Then, when you add on the responsibility of overseeing all of the university's other outdoor athletics facilities, including baseball's Eck Stadium, soccer's Alumni Field, and lacrosse's Moose Krause Stadium, Brazo's duties could be overwhelming. He is quick to point out it would not be possible without the assistance of his veteran crew, which averages more than 10 years of experience per man.

"We couldn't begin to do any of the things we do with the facilities here at Notre Dame without an exceptional crew," Brazo says. "I'm so appreciative of the job they do on a daily basis. Their experience and knowledge is something you can't replace, and I've been fortunate to have had to hire just one full-time person in my entire time here at Notre Dame."

Brazo is a 1971 graduate of Michigan State, where he earned his bachelor's degree in biology. Two years later, he received his master's degree in the same discipline, and in 1989, he added a

Ph.D. in biology. In addition, prior to coming to Notre Dame in 1992, Brazo was a research associate and instructor in the department of natural resources at Michigan State.

In 1999 Brazo assumed various duties associated with the development and environmental impact of the new Warren Golf Course, located on the north side of the Notre Dame campus. In August 2000 he stepped into his current role as the manager of all athletics facilities at Notre Dame, while continuing to serve as an instructor in turf grass management at Andrews University through 2002.

"I guess that between going to Michigan State and all the time I've spent working with these facilities and the environment, you could probably say my favorite color is green—with a lot of blue mixed in!" Brazo says with a laugh.

"In all seriousness," he continued, "with all the growth in the world's population and the rise in the production of chemicals and pollution in our society, I think we all have a responsibility to be more environmentally aware. That's what we try to use as a guideline when we address any facility management problems here at Notre Dame. Education is our biggest focus, and we look to put that into practice in our facilities."

Ironically, Brazo is the first to admit that when it comes to his yard at home in Niles, Michigan, it doesn't exactly match up with Notre Dame Stadium.

"I'd guess my home backyard is probably the worst in the neighborhood," he chuckles. "But after you spend as much time as we do working on the turf at the stadium and at other facilities on campus, the last thing you want to do when you get home is turn around and work on your own lawn."

One would guess Brazo's neighbors will give him a free pass on his yard, especially in light of the hard work and energy expended by Brazo in making Notre Dame's facilities among the best in the country.

Play Like a Champion Today

It's just a simple wooden sign, painted gold and blue and mounted on a cream-colored brick wall at the foot of a stairwell. Yet, the "Play Like A Champion Today" sign, found outside Notre Dame's locker room, is so much more.

The slogan "Play Like A Champion Today" is so synonymous with the university that one can be excused for believing that Father Edward Sorin, the school's founder, received it as a divine revelation in 1842.

While the exact origin of the slogan is not known, the sign that currently hangs in Notre Dame Stadium came courtesy of former coach Lou Holtz.

"I read a lot of books about the history of Notre Dame and its football program," Holtz explains. "I forget which book I was looking at—it had an old picture in it that showed the slogan 'Play Like A Champion Today.'

"I said, 'That is really appropriate; it used to be at Notre Dame and we need to use it again.' So, I had that sign made up."

Soon, the tradition of hitting the sign before every game developed. Holtz even used a copy of the sign when traveling to road contests to help motivate the team. The players took no time in embracing Holtz's idea.

"[The players] were encouraged by it," Holtz says. "I told them the history of it, that this had been here years ago. I didn't know who took it down, I don't know why it wasn't here when I came here, but this is part of Notre Dame tradition and this is what we're going to do.

"Hopefully, it will be here for years to come."

Chances are, it will—the sign still inspires the same feelings that Holtz hoped it would back in 1986.

"[Whenever I see it] I think 'Why not? Why not today? Why not this game? Why not right now?'" Irish tackle Ryan Harris says. "You just remember what you're out here to do. You came to Notre

Dame to be a champion, and every time I see it, I think 'Why not? Let's go do it!' "

Former quarterback/receiver Carlyle Holiday vividly remembers his first encounter with the famous sign. "The first time I hit it, Anthony Denman, who was a linebacker here, said, 'When you hit it, you better mean it,' " Holiday recalls. "The guys take it seriously, so it meant a lot to me. I knew you had to come out with intensity when you hit that sign."

As Holiday's Notre Dame career came to a close, the slogan took on a special meaning.

"You know that the time is coming when you won't be able to hit that sign for very long," he says, "so you've got to take advantage of it and cherish every moment you get to hit that sign when coming down the tunnel."

Former Irish coach Gerry Faust, a great believer in motivational tools, has spoken to the team at various times and believes in the power of the "Champion" message.

"The word *champion* means you're the best—the very definition of it," Faust says. "You're a bar above the rest. When you play that way, you're going to be the best. And if you give your best, that's all you can ask of a person."

To Holtz—the man who resurrected what has become even a worldwide phenomenon—the hitting of the sign comes with a solemn commitment.

"Regardless of the win-loss record, regardless of the problems you have," Holtz says, "when you walk out on that field you have an obligation to your teammates and the fans to play to the best of your ability—to play like a champion and to think like a champion.

"But, I also asked my players that every time they hit that sign, to think about all the sacrifices your family has made; your teammates made in high school; the sacrifices your teachers have made; and you also think of the thousands of people who would love to be in your position. Just think about how fortunate we are.

"All of these thoughts should go through your mind when you hit that sign—'Play Like A Champion Today.' "

Scroope and Notre Dame Football Are a Perfect Fit

Of all the symbols associated with the Notre Dame football program, perhaps none is as universally recognized as the gold helmet, with its modest look and nary a logo to be found.

The responsibility of maintaining not only those famed gold helmets, but every other piece of football equipment as well, is held by head equipment manager Henry Scroope. He is charged with making sure every Notre Dame football player is safely protected when he takes the field, while also preserving the high standards of appearance that go along with being a member of the Fighting Irish.

"The most important part of my job is the protection of our student-athletes," Scroope says. "Part of my certification as an equipment manager involves going through continuing education on the latest developments in all types of gear. We make sure our players take the field in the best equipment possible so they are well protected and equipped to play their best."

Scroope has been associated with Notre Dame athletics for the better part of the past two decades. A native of Staten Island, New York, he enrolled at the university in 1993 and began working on his bachelor's degree in government. A three-sport athlete in high school, Scroope wanted to continue his athletic career in college and found the best means to do that was through the Notre Dame athletic student manager program.

Unlike any manager program of its kind in the country, the Notre Dame model provides support for virtually every athletic team on campus. Midway through their freshmen year, students at both Notre Dame and Saint Mary's are invited to participate in the manager program, with approximately 100 to 150 students signing on as sophomores to work with the Irish football team. Primarily, they work with football game preparation, including painting the omnipresent gold helmets each week.

After their sophomore years, the managers go through a peer evaluation, with the top 21 candidates being invited back for another year with the football program. The process repeats at the

The plain gold helmets worn by the Fighting Irish are among the most iconic symbols in American sports, and, like all other Notre Dame gear, they are religiously protected and maintained by equipment manager Henry Scroope. Photo courtesy of AP/Wide World Images.

end of the following football season, with the top three students being designated "senior managers," while the remaining students may choose which of the other Irish athletic teams they would like to work with during their senior year.

Scroope went through this process himself and in 1996 was selected as a senior manager in charge of personnel as a member of Lou Holtz's final Notre Dame team. It was a process that had a significant effect on Scroope's life.

"Being a manager taught me a great deal of responsibility, as well as how to interact with different groups of people," he says.

After graduating from Notre Dame in May 1997, Scroope returned home to Staten Island, where he spent time as the assistant manager at Silver Lake Golf Course and later became the marketing and promotions coordinator at Wagner College. However, Notre Dame remained his first love, and in 1999 he jumped at the chance to fill the vacant position of assistant equipment manager for the Irish.

A year later, Scroope moved into his current position as the head of the football equipment operation at Notre Dame. It also brought his journey full circle, as he now oversees the very same student manager program that he enjoyed so much. Since his promotion, Scroope has been proactive in the area of student-athlete safety, serving on the Schutt Safety Council in 2002 and 2003 while helping the helmet manufacturer come up with new methods of head gear protection.

Somewhere in the midst of his varied responsibilities at Notre Dame, Scroope found time to marry his college sweetheart, Maggie, in July of 2003. In fact, the wedding coincided with a unique job opportunity for Scroope—the chance to work as an assistant in the American League clubhouse at the 2003 Major League Baseball All-Star Game at U.S. Cellular Field in Chicago. The game itself was just three days after Scroope's wedding, and he is the first to admit it took a very understanding spouse to pull off such an arrangement.

"I'm very fortunate to have someone like Maggie who loves sports as much as I do," Scroope says. "She had as great a time at the All-Star Game as I did, and we were able to go on our honeymoon after the game. I think that was probably one of the greatest weeks I've ever experienced."

The marriage of Scroope with the Notre Dame football program has been equally great. In fact, you might say that it's a perfect fit—just like a gold helmet.

Film at 11: Collins Keeps Irish on Cutting Edge of Video Technology

When the final gun sounds each Saturday during the fall, Tim Collins's job is just getting started.

The full-time video systems technician for the Notre Dame athletics department, Collins is in charge of all video and filming needs for the Irish football, basketball, and hockey teams. In addition to filming all Notre Dame football games and practices, he is responsible for compiling all of the video packages used by the Irish football coaches in their scouting and game preparation.

A native of South Bend, Collins first began working at Notre Dame on a part-time basis in 1988 following his graduation from

John Adams High School. That first year turned out to be a pretty good one for the Irish, who went undefeated and claimed the school's 11th national championship. At the time, the Notre Dame video department still shot many of the football team's practices and games on a mix of VHS tape and 16-millimeter film.

"Back then, it would take us the better part of a day to get the film edited and ready for the coaches to view," Collins says. "I was pretty well-versed in VHS and Beta filming, which we started to use in 1988, so it made the transition a little smoother for us."

Besides his part-time duties at Notre Dame, Collins spent three years as a news photographer at WNDU-TV in South Bend. When the Irish athletics department came calling with a full-time position, he quickly accepted and soon settled into a small office tucked under the stands at Notre Dame Stadium.

"It was pretty amazing to be able to go to work at Notre Dame Stadium each day," he says. "Being here for as long as I have, sometimes you take for granted what a special place Notre Dame is, but it has come to mean more and more to me as I get older."

Under Collins's guidance, the Notre Dame athletics video department has evolved into a state-of-the-art operation, complete with enough new technology and computer equipment to put several NFL teams to shame. Using Sony Betacam SX cameras, Collins and his six-person crew employ a full nonlinear editing system that allows complete film of a game or practice to be downloaded to a computer and ready for use within one hour. In fact, once the film's contents are placed on a computer hard drive, the videotape itself will no longer exist, a feature that would have been nearly unthinkable just 15 years ago.

With the football team's move into the Guglielmino Athletics Complex prior to the 2005 season, Collins now oversees a state-of-the-art system that resides right in the middle of all the Irish coaching offices.

Steve Horvath, a part-time member of the Notre Dame video staff since 1958, says Collins's professional demeanor sets him apart.

"He does such a great job keeping everything organized and prepared," Horvath observes. "Tim is a good guy to work for because he's so straightforward and direct with you."

In June 2004 the Notre Dame Monogram Club recognized Collins for his years of service by awarding him an honorary monogram. It was an honor that took the then-35-year-old by surprise.

"There are people who work here all their lives and don't receive something as big as that," Collins says. "I was shocked when I found out about it because I thought you had to be retired first."

So when the Notre Dame players walk to the student section following games and raise their helmets in a gilded salute, remember that they are not only honoring their fellow classmates and supporters, but also the hard work of people like Tim Collins who made this weekend's performance possible.

Notre Dame Student-Athletes Learn from Sarge's Message

"*Selfless* is a word that comes to mind. He's somebody who you know would have your back if you were in trouble. He's just a great friend," Pat Holmes, Notre Dame's director of Academic Services for Student-Athletes, says.

Holmes isn't describing a college roommate of his or a friend he's had since childhood. He is, in fact, describing Notre Dame academic counselor Adam Sargent, a man he's known on a personal and professional level for only the past seven years.

He is describing the same Adam Sargent who, after turning down schools like Princeton and Duke, wore the blue and gold of Notre Dame on the lacrosse field every day for three years, helping the Irish to three NCAA tournament appearances, before it all came to, literally, a crashing end.

At about 8:30 on the morning of May 29, 1997, Sargent was on his way to Saint Mary's College to take an education test when he was involved in a two-car accident at the intersection of Notre

Dame Avenue and Angela Boulevard. The accident left the Rochester, New York, native paralyzed from the chest down, and unsure of what lay ahead.

"The first thing that went through my mind was the question of what I was going to be able to do, and whether or not I was going to be able to continue being an independent and self-made person," Sargent says.

Following a three-month stint at the Rehabilitation Institute of Chicago, Sargent, or "Sarge," as he is affectionately known, returned to his hometown and began to adjust to his new lifestyle.

"There was certainly the fear of going from a healthy 21-year-old to someone who is now potentially dependent on other people. There was fear, but there was also hope that I could become an independent, productive person again," he says.

Sargent turned that hope into a reality the following January, when he returned to campus and began taking classes toward his Notre Dame degree. In the spring of '99, he graduated from the university with a double major in history and anthropology.

After his graduation, however, Sargent realized that more uncertainty was in store as he pondered the next step in his life.

"I was going to go to [the University of] Virginia for a master's program, but I wasn't sure that that was what I wanted to do. I was fortunate enough to get an internship in Academic Services, and I decided to remain at Notre Dame," Sargent says.

For Sargent, that internship turned into a full-time job, and he has spent the past seven years as a counselor in Notre Dame's Academic Services department.

"Adam brings so many positives to our office that it's difficult to list them all," Holmes says. "He's passionate about what he does, and it's very obvious that he loves what he does. Having been a student-athlete at Notre Dame, he understands the situation. He's quick to recognize when he should push someone and when he should back off, which is important in this job."

Currently Sargent serves as the academic counselor for the Irish football squad, after previously working with a handful of other Notre Dame teams.

Head men's lacrosse coach Kevin Corrigan, who coached Sargent as a player and calls him "one of my heroes," is quick to echo Holmes's sentiments about the job Sargent does with the student-athletes in his charge.

"Sarge has a great combination of empathy and determination to get things done," Corrigan says. "He's got a great 'BS detector.' He knows when people aren't putting forth full effort, and he doesn't take excuses very often. I've been with Sarge in the best of times and the worst of times, and I've never been anything but impressed with him. He's a great positive influence for any of the athletes at this university."

While that influence is felt by Notre Dame athletes on a daily basis, it isn't, however, limited to the campus.

In addition to his duties in the Academic Services department, Sargent spends his Thursday afternoons at St. Joseph's Hospital, working with patients who are referred for psychotherapy, as part of the master's of counseling degree he received from Indiana University–South Bend in May of 2004.

"Once I started that program and got to work with a different population of people, I really enjoyed it. It's been a great opportunity for me and it's something that will probably become a bigger part of my life as things continue," Sargent says.

Ironically, Sargent credits his accident with helping him develop the interpersonal skills he utilizes every day in his occupational and counseling endeavors.

"Before the accident, much of what I did to define myself was done in the physical world," Sargent says. "After much of that was significantly reduced, I started to cultivate the social, interpersonal, and intellectual parts of me that had always been there. As more and more people start to trust you, it's your responsibility to develop those skills."

For the countless people who Sargent has influenced and affected during his tenure in the Academic Services department, the accident that happened on that otherwise ordinary spring day in 1997 could also be seen as a blessing. The reason is, simply, that Sargent may have never started working in his current position without those certain circumstances.

"I honestly don't know what path I would've chosen. I pictured myself possibly doing some sort of teaching in the long run. I definitely wouldn't have developed the skills I have now as quickly as I did because there are other things that I would've given greater attention to," he says.

Without a doubt, there is a multitude of people in both the Notre Dame community and the South Bend area that, at the mere mention of Sargent's name, will burst into a smile and praise the man who has given them so much of himself without asking for anything in return.

Football Announcer Punches It Up

"Who wants to listen to a policeman telling everyone to behave themselves?" Tim McCarthy asked himself. He knew the answer.

The year was 1960, and McCarthy had just been promoted from trooper in the Indiana State Police to safety education sergeant. One of his new responsibilities was to make an announcement at Notre Dame home football games reminding people to drive safely on the way home, but after two games he knew people weren't paying attention.

He decided to change that by adding something to the message.

At the first home game in 1961, the message was about drinking and driving, and McCarthy ended by saying, "The automobile replaced the horse, but the driver should stay on the wagon."

Several hundred stadium announcements later, fans in Notre Dame Stadium fall silent in eager anticipation during the fourth quarter when they hear, "May I have your attention, please. This is Tim McCarthy for the Indiana State Police."

They know what's coming: a reminder to drive carefully and courteously on the way home, punctuated by an often groan-inducing play on words.

McCarthy says he got the wordplay idea from a friend of his, Chicago police officer Glen Baldy, who used the device in the helicopter traffic reports he did for a radio station. Baldy gave McCarthy a few ideas to try at the Notre Dame games.

After running through these and receiving a good response, it was up to McCarthy to keep the tradition alive.

Early on, the safety sergeant worried that the gag might be taken as trivializing the hard and dangerous work the state police perform, so he reverted to announcing the messages straight. But fans kept asking for the punch lines. McCarthy says he knew then that if he reinstated the punch lines, fans would listen more closely than ever.

These days when he makes the announcements McCarthy identifies himself as "for" the Indiana State Police rather than "of" because he retired from the force in December 1978 after being elected sheriff of Porter County. He later was appointed county tax assessor. In 1999 he retired from political life to form his own company, which does tax appraisal work for assessors.

In recent years, McCarthy has made a number of appearances at Notre Dame football pep rallies and luncheons and other events, delivering his trademark introduction and remarks. Ironically, most Irish fans recognized his voice, but they had no idea what he looked like.

He admits he still gets the jitters when he steps up to the mic. He says it's not easy coming up with new plays on words, so he keeps an ear out for them throughout the year. He gets a kick out of fans' reactions and says he doesn't mind when the lines aren't met with applause.

"I've been booed a few times," he says, 'but that's okay because I knew they listened to the safety announcement."

The Man behind the Mike

How many of us get to live out our childhood dream? Probably not many of us do, but one person who does is Notre Dame Stadium public address announcer Mike Collins. He gets his chance with every Irish home football game.

Delivering Irish football fans all the important facts and figures from high above the stadium in the fourth level of the press box, Collins is living the dream that started when he was just a kid in Pittsburgh, Pennsylvania.

"Believe it or not, I always wanted to be a PA announcer. Some people want to be firemen or policemen, but from the first sporting event I ever attended, being a stadium public address announcer is what I wanted to do," says Collins.

The dream started with his first visit to a major league baseball park.

"My father took me to my first Pittsburgh Pirates game at Forbes Field when I was five or six," Collins recalls. "We got there early and were sitting in our seats when, all of a sudden, I heard this voice echo through the park. I said to my dad, 'Where's that coming from?' He said, 'Well, it's coming from back there [pointing in the direction of the press box].' And I thought right then and there that was one of the coolest things. I hate to say this but, I remember that as a little kid, I used to practice being a baseball PA announcer at home."

Little did Collins know then, but the voice he heard at that first baseball game would play a key role in his dream job many years later. As fate would have it, he didn't get to become a baseball PA announcer, but he's very happy in his role at Notre Dame.

"I consider it one of the cream of the crop jobs in stadium announcing around the country, along with places like Yankee Stadium, Dodger Stadium, and Giants Stadium. And, of course, the Pittsburgh Steelers and Pittsburgh Pirates."

A 1967 graduate of Notre Dame with a degree in communications, Collins is well known to local fans as a news anchor on WSBT-TV in South Bend. He got his start as a PA announcer with the Notre Dame hockey team in the late 1970s, a role he continued until just a few years ago. When the chance to become the football PA announcer came up, the enthusiastic Collins didn't have to be asked twice.

"Frank Crosiar was the longtime PA announcer for Notre Dame football and was considering retiring. Roger Valdiserri— then the Notre Dame sports information director—told me if he did retire, he would give me the chance to audition," says Collins. "Frank decided to retire a week before the start of the 1982 season. Roger called me on the Thursday before the opening game and asked me if I wanted to do the game on Saturday. I said, 'Do you mean the football game?' and he said, 'Yes, Frank has decided to retire, can you do it?' and I said, 'Sure.'"

With little time to prepare for his first game behind the stadium mike, Collins got pointers from Crosiar and that voice from his past—longtime Pirates public address announcer Art McKennan.

"I got in touch with Mr. McKennan through the Pirates. I told him how much I admired the way he handled the job and asked if he had any advice for me. He said a couple of things to me. First was, 'Remember, no one is paying a dime of their ticket price to listen to the PA announcer and always keep that in mind. You're there to help the fans, to be professional, and to be enthusiastic in what you are doing. If you keep that in mind and don't try to be a comedian or some kind of hotshot up there, you'll do fine.'"

As it turned out, Collins's first game would be a historic one—the first-ever night game at Notre Dame Stadium. The Irish defeated Michigan 23–17 in a nationally televised game, and the veteran announcer smiles when he looks back on the events that started his dream job.

"I guess I had the chance to embarrass myself in front of 60,000 fans and, if it was loud enough, millions of people around the country. Everything worked out, we didn't make many mistakes, and I was absolutely thrilled to be doing it," says Collins.

There's also lots of work and preparation that goes into getting ready for each Saturday's home game.

"I would say I spend several hours a week on preparation for each game. I try to know as much about the Notre Dame players going into the season and then work on each week's opponent," says Collins. "On game day, I have a routine that starts two hours prior to kickoff. I set everything up in the booth the way I want it. My charts, my media guides, the game announcements—I read them over and edit them. I'll meet with the opponent's sports information office to go over pronunciations and changes. Being well prepared helps me get relaxed. My job starts about two minutes before the Notre Dame team comes on the field. From there, you're on the go for three and a half hours."

Collins came to South Bend for college in 1963 with an interest in journalism. He got involved with WSND, the student radio station, while also spending time at the local television stations WSBT and WNDU doing a variety of jobs to gain experience.

As would be the case with his public address job, his first job in broadcasting was a result of being in the right place at the right time.

"I was just out of college a couple of months and working at WNDU. Two of the news anchors left within days of each other. I was doing radio at the time, and they asked me if I could anchor the news that night. I said yes. After about four months, they decided to keep me," says the veteran newsman.

During his years high above the stadium turf, Collins has seen great Irish teams, great opponents, and some great games. Among his all-time favorites were the 1988 win over top-ranked Miami on the way to that undefeated season and national championship, the 1993 win over number one Florida State, and the visits from Penn State during the 1980s and early '90s.

For Collins, the job as Notre Dame PA announcer isn't a job, it's a labor of love. He goes into every game with a simple philosophy that has carried him a long way.

"I've always thought that a good PA announcer should be like a good game official. If they didn't get in the way, you know they've done a good job at the end of the game," says Collins.

Collins's contributions earned him an honorary monogram from the Notre Dame Monogram Club, presented at halftime of the final 2006 Irish home game.

sources

Chapter 1

Rockne: A Line for Every Occasion
All Rockne quotes from
Heisler, John. *Quotable Rockne*. Nashville: TowleHouse Publishing, 2001.

Rockne: The Coach and the Car
Kish, Bernie. "Rockne: The Coach and the Car." *Notre Dame Football GameDay Magazine*. November 12, 2005. Notre Dame vs. Navy.

Chapter 2

Catching Up With...Mike Layden
Kleppel, Ken. "Catching Up With...Mike Layden." *Notre Dame Football GameDay Magazine*. September 17, 2005. Notre Dame vs. Michigan State.

Chapter 3

Angelo Bertelli: Pioneer of a Tradition
Somogyi, Lou. "Angelo Bertelli: Pioneer of a Tradition." *Notre Dame Football GameDay Magazine*. September 9, 2006. Notre Dame vs. Penn State.

Memorable Moment: Bertelli's Final Game
Somogyi, Lou. "Memorable Moment: Bertelli's Final Game." *Notre Dame Football GameDay Magazine*. September 9, 2006. Notre Dame vs. Penn State.

The Ultimate Notre Dame Player/Man
Somogyi, Lou. "The Ultimate Notre Dame Player/Man." *Notre Dame Football GameDay Magazine*. September 16, 2006. Notre Dame vs. Michigan.

10 Questions with John Lujack
Somogyi, Lou. "10 Questions with John Lujack." *Notre Dame Football GameDay Magazine*. September 16, 2006. Notre Dame vs. Michigan.

Zygmont Always Left Them Laughing
"It's too crowded after practice..."
"I don't know if they'll feed me..."
"Thanks, General. And speaking for..."

"Hold it, Coach..."
Bonifer, Michael, and L.G. Weaver. *Out of Bounds: An Anecdotal History of Notre Dame Football.* Easton, CT: Piper Publishing, Inc., 1978.

Catching Up With...Frank and Kelly Tripucka
Chval, Craig. "Catching Up With...Frank and Kelly Tripucka." *Notre Dame Football GameDay Magazine.* November 19, 2005. Notre Dame vs. Syracuse.

You Gotta Have Hart
Somogyi, Lou. "You Gotta Have Hart." *Notre Dame Football GameDay Magazine.* October 7, 2006. Notre Dame vs. Stanford.

10 Questions with Kevin Hart
Somogyi, Lou. "10 Questions with Kevin Hart." *Notre Dame Football GameDay Magazine.* October 7, 2006. Notre Dame vs. Stanford.

Pulling Double Duty
Somogyi, Lou. "Pulling Double Duty." *Notre Dame Football GameDay Magazine.* October 7, 2006. Notre Dame vs. Stanford.

Catching Up With...Jerry Groom
Kleppel, Ken. "Catching Up With...Jerry Groom." *Notre Dame Football GameDay Magazine.* October 15, 2005. Notre Dame vs. USC.

From Cruiser to Aircraft Carrier: John Lattner
Somogyi, Lou. "From Cruiser to Aircraft Carrier: John Lattner." *Notre Dame Football GameDay Magazine.* September 30, 2006. Notre Dame vs. Purdue.

10 Questions with John Lattner
Somogyi, Lou. "10 Questions with John Lattner." *Notre Dame Football GameDay Magazine.* September 30, 2006. Notre Dame vs. Purdue.

Fumble Recovery
Somogyi, Lou. "Fumble Recovery." *Notre Dame Football GameDay Magazine.* September 30, 2006. Notre Dame vs. Purdue.

Golden Memories: The 1953 Notre Dame Team
Chval, Craig. "Golden Memories: The 1953 Notre Dame Team." *Notre Dame Football GameDay Magazine.* November 8, 2003. Notre Dame vs. Navy.

Chapter 4

Catching Up With...Terry Brennan
Chval, Craig. "Catching Up With...Terry Brennan." *Notre Dame Football GameDay Magazine.* November 18, 2006. Notre Dame vs. Army.

Golden Anniversary for the Golden Boy
Somogyi, Lou. "Golden Anniversary for the Golden Boy." *Notre Dame Football GameDay Magazine.* October 20, 2006. Notre Dame vs. UCLA.

Chapter 5

Magical 1964 Season Marked Debut of Era of Ara

LaFleur, Pete. "Magical 1964 Season Marked Debut of Era of Ara." *Notre Dame Football GameDay Magazine.* October 9, 2004. Notre Dame vs. Stanford.

Ara, Can You Really Stop That Snow?

"That's ridiculous. Do you think…"

"Do you think I should…"

Pagna, Tom, with Bob Best. *Notre Dame's Era of Ara.* South Bend, IN: Diamond Communications, 1976.

John Huarte: Timing Matters

Somogyi, Lou. "John Huarte: Timing Matters." *Notre Dame Football GameDay Magazine.* November 4, 2006. Notre Dame vs. North Carolina.

10 Questions with John Huarte

Somogyi, Lou. "10 Questions with John Huarte." *Notre Dame Football GameDay Magazine.* November 4, 2006. Notre Dame vs. North Carolina.

Remembering Dick Arrington

"If I were going to go to college…"

"When people ask me how…"

"You have to have knowledge in the first place…"

"Everyone is basically lazy…"

Bettag, Tom, and Mike Bradley. "Athlete of the Year." *The Scholastic* (May 28, 1965).

"The moment Dick Arrington started…"

"After our game against California…"

"As we noticed on film…"

Parseghian, Ara. "Switch in Time Saves Defensive Line." *Chicago Sun-Times* (October 5, 1965).

Catching Up With…Larry Conjar

Chval, Craig. "Catching Up With…Larry Conjar." *Notre Dame Football GameDay Magazine.* November 5, 2005. Notre Dame vs. Tennessee.

Catching Up With…Jim Lynch

Chval, Craig. "Catching Up With…Jim Lynch." *Notre Dame Football GameDay Magazine.* November 12, 2005. Notre Dame vs. Navy.

Catching Up With…George Goeddeke

Chval, Craig. "Catching Up With…George Goeddeke." *Notre Dame Football GameDay Magazine.* October 2, 2004. Notre Dame vs. Purdue.

From Gridiron to Supreme Court: Page and Thomas Still Making a Difference
Kleppel, Ken. "From Gridiron to Supreme Court: Page and Thomas Still Making a Difference." *Notre Dame Football GameDay Magazine.* November 5, 2005. Notre Dame vs. Tennessee.

Catching Up With...Bob Gladieux
Chval, Craig. "Catching Up With...Bob Gladieux." *Notre Dame Football GameDay Magazine.* September 17, 2005. Notre Dame vs. Michigan State.

Catching Up With...Coley O'Brien
Chval, Craig. "Catching Up With...Coley O'Brien." *Notre Dame Football GameDay Magazine.* October 22, 2005. Notre Dame vs. BYU.

Catching Up With...Mr. Fling (Terry Hanratty) and Mr. Cling (Jim Seymour)
Chval, Craig. "Catching Up With...Mr. Fling (Terry Hanratty) and Mr. Cling (Jim Seymour)." *Notre Dame Football GameDay Magazine.* October 2, 2004. Notre Dame vs. Purdue.

Catching Up With...Mike McCoy
Chval, Craig. "Catching Up With...Mike McCoy." *Notre Dame Football GameDay Magazine.* October 23, 2004. Notre Dame vs. Boston College.

Catching Up With...Walt Patulski
Chval, Craig. "Catching Up With...Walt Patulski." *Notre Dame Football GameDay Magazine.* September 25, 2004. Notre Dame vs. Washington.

Catching Up With...Roger Valdiserri
Chval, Craig. "Catching Up With...Roger Valdiserri." *Notre Dame Football GameDay Magazine.* September 25, 2004. Notre Dame vs. Washington.

Yesterday's Heroes: Clarence Ellis
Kleppel, Ken. "Yesterday's Heroes: Clarence Ellis." *Notre Dame Football GameDay Magazine.* October 22, 2005. Notre Dame vs. BYU.

Catching Up With...Tom Gatewood
Chval, Craig. "Catching Up With...Tom Gatewood." *Notre Dame Football GameDay Magazine.* October 9, 2004. Notre Dame vs. Stanford.

Catching Up With...Greg Marx
Chval, Craig. "Catching Up With...Greg Marx." *Notre Dame Football GameDay Magazine.* October 15, 2005. Notre Dame vs. USC.

Irish Football 1973: Changes Bring About a Championship
Chval, Craig. "Irish Football 1973: Changes Bring About a Championship." *Notre Dame Football GameDay Magazine.* October 18, 2003. Notre Dame vs. USC.

Catching Up With...Mike Townsend
Chval, Craig. "Catching Up With...Mike Townsend." *Notre Dame Football GameDay Magazine.* October 9, 2004. Notre Dame vs. Stanford.

Catching Up With...Gary Potempa
Chval, Craig. "Catching Up With...Gary Potempa." *Notre Dame Football GameDay Magazine.* October 15, 2005. Notre Dame vs. USC.

Catching Up With...Wayne Bullock
Chval, Craig. "Catching Up With...Wayne Bullock." *Notre Dame Football GameDay Magazine.* November 4, 2006. Notre Dame vs. North Carolina.

Yesterday's Heroes: Steve Niehaus
LaFleur, Pete. "Yesterday's Heroes: Steve Niehaus." *Notre Dame Football GameDay Magazine.* November 5, 2005. Notre Dame vs. Tennessee.

Catching Up With...Robin Weber
Chval, Craig. "Catching Up With...Robin Weber." *Notre Dame Football GameDay Magazine.* October 21, 2006. Notre Dame vs. UCLA.

Chapter 6

Catching Up With...Ken MacAfee
Chval, Craig. "Catching Up With...Ken MacAfee." *Notre Dame Football GameDay Magazine.* October 23, 2004. Notre Dame vs. Boston College.

Catching Up With...Kris Haines
Chval, Craig. "Catching Up With...Kris Haines." *Notre Dame Football GameDay Magazine.* September 11, 2004. Notre Dame vs. Michigan.

Catching Up With...Luther Bradley
Chval, Craig. "Catching Up With...Luther Bradley." *Notre Dame Football GameDay Magazine.* November 12, 2005. Notre Dame vs. Navy.

Catching Up With...Ted Burgmeier
Chval, Craig. "Catching Up With...Ted Burgmeier." *Notre Dame Football GameDay Magazine.* October 7, 2006. Notre Dame vs. Stanford.

The Comeback Kid: Joe Montana
"The guys on the team knew..."
Zimmerman, Paul. "The Ultimate Winner." *Sports Illustrated* (August 13, 1990).

Catching Up With...Jerome Heavens
Chval, Craig. "Catching Up With...Jerome Heavens." *Notre Dame Football GameDay Magazine.* November 4, 2006. Notre Dame vs. North Carolina.

Catching Up With…Chuck Male
Chval, Craig. "Catching Up With…Chuck Male." *Notre Dame Football GameDay Magazine.* September 16, 2006. Notre Dame vs. Michigan.

Catching Up With…John Scully
Chval, Craig. "Catching Up With…John Scully." *Notre Dame Football GameDay Magazine.* October 9, 2004. Notre Dame vs. Stanford.

Catching Up With…Tom Gibbons
Chval, Craig. "Catching Up With…Tom Gibbons." *Notre Dame Football GameDay Magazine.* November 5, 2005. Notre Dame vs. Tennessee.

Catching Up With…Jim Stone
Chval, Craig. "Catching Up With…Jim Stone." *Notre Dame Football GameDay Magazine.* November 18, 2006. Notre Dame vs. Army.

Chapter 7

Harry Oliver: The Unlikely Hero
"It wasn't a good start…"
"You know, just as I placed…"
"This was the all-time…"
"I couldn't look…"
Jauss, Bill. "Irish Kicker Sends Michigan into the Wind." *Chicago Tribune* (September 21, 1980).
"I've never seen Harry kick one…"
"I didn't look up until…"
Marquard, Bill. "A Nifty Twist by Oliver." *Irish Eyes* (March 1, 1981).

Catching Up With…Phil Carter
Chval, Craig. "Catching Up With…Phil Carter." *Notre Dame Football GameDay Magazine.* September 17, 2005. Notre Dame vs. Michigan State.

Catching Up With…Tom Thayer
Chval, Craig. "Catching Up With…Tom Thayer." *Notre Dame Football GameDay Magazine.* October 15, 2005. Notre Dame vs. USC.

Catching Up With…Tim Scannell
Chval, Craig. "Catching Up With…Tim Scannell." *Notre Dame Football GameDay Magazine.* October 22, 2005. Notre Dame vs. BYU.

Chapter 8

Tim Brown: Victorious Amid Defeat
Somogyi, Lou. "Tim Brown: Victorious Amid Defeat." *Notre Dame Football GameDay Magazine.* November 17, 2006. Notre Dame vs. Army.

Catching Up With...Darrell "Flash" Gordon

Kleppel, Ken. "Catching Up With...Darrell 'Flash' Gordon." *Notre Dame Football GameDay Magazine.* November 12, 2005. Notre Dame vs. Navy.

Catching Up With...Reggie Ho

Chval, Craig. "Catching Up With...Reggie Ho." *Notre Dame Football GameDay Magazine.* September 11, 2004. Notre Dame vs. Michigan.

Catching Up With...The Three Amigos: Legendary Linebackers Wes Pritchett, Michael Stonebreaker, and Frank Stams

Chval, Craig. "Catching Up With...The Three Amigos: Legendary Linebackers Wes Pritchett, Michael Stonebreaker, and Frank Stams." *Notre Dame Football GameDay Magazine.* November 13, 2004. Notre Dame vs. Pittsburgh.

Catching Up With...Ned Bolcar

Chval, Craig. "Catching Up With...Ned Bolcar." *Notre Dame Football GameDay Magazine.* September 16, 2006. Notre Dame vs. Michigan.

Catching Up With...Tim Grunhard

Chval, Craig. "Catching Up With...Tim Grunhard." *Notre Dame Football GameDay Magazine.* October 21, 2006. Notre Dame vs. UCLA.

Catching Up With...Reggie Brooks

Chval, Craig. "Catching Up With...Reggie Brooks." *Notre Dame Football GameDay Magazine.* September 11, 2004. Notre Dame vs. Michigan.

Catching Up With...Rick Mirer

Chval, Craig. "Catching Up With...Rick Mirer." *Notre Dame Football GameDay Magazine.* September 16, 2006. Notre Dame vs. Michigan.

Catching Up With...Kevin McDougal

Chval, Craig. "Catching Up With...Kevin McDougal." *Notre Dame Football GameDay Magazine.* October 23, 2004. Notre Dame vs. Boston College.

Catching Up With...Devon McDonald

Chval, Craig. "Catching Up With...Devon McDonald." *Notre Dame Football GameDay Magazine.* September 30, 2006. Notre Dame vs. Purdue.

Chapter 9

Yesterday's Heroes: Kory Minor

Kleppel, Ken. "Yesterday's Heroes: Kory Minor." *Notre Dame Football GameDay Magazine.* November 19, 2005. Notre Dame vs. Syracuse.

Catching Up With...Jim Sanson

Chval, Craig. "Catching Up With...Jim Sanson." *Notre Dame Football GameDay Magazine*. September 25, 2004. Notre Dame vs. Washington.

Chapter 10

Green Is Good for Brazo and Irish

Masters, Chris. "Green Is Good for Brazo and Irish." *Notre Dame Football GameDay Magazine*. November 13, 2004. Notre Dame vs. Pittsburgh.

Play Like a Champion Today

Touney, Greg. "Play Like a Champion Today." *Notre Dame Football GameDay Magazine*. November 13, 2004. Notre Dame vs. Pittsburgh.

Scroope and Notre Dame Football Are a Perfect Fit

Masters, Chris. "Scroope and Notre Dame Football Are a Perfect Fit." *Notre Dame Football GameDay Magazine*. October 23, 2004. Notre Dame vs. Boston College.

Film at 11: Collins Keeps Irish on Cutting Edge of Video Technology

Masters, Chris. "Film at 11: Collins Keeps Irish on Cutting Edge of Video Technology." *Notre Dame Football GameDay Magazine*. October 9, 2004. Notre Dame vs. Stanford.

Notre Dame Student-Athletes Learn from Sarge's Message

Walton, Cory. "Notre Dame Student-Athletes Learn from Sarge's Message." *Notre Dame Football GameDay Magazine*. September 25, 2004. Notre Dame vs. Washington.

Football Announcer Punches It Up

Katzmann, Kristy. "Football Announcer Punches It Up." *Notre Dame Magazine*. Autumn 2000.

The Man Behind the Mike

Connor, Tim. "The Man Behind the Mike." *Notre Dame Football GameDay Magazine*. October 13, 2001. Notre Dame vs. West Virginia.